HEPTAGON
WRITINGS

EDUCATION
INNOVATION
WORK
IMMIGRATION
TRADE
CHINA
AMERICA

HEPTAGON
WRITINGS

Over Fifty Years of National and Geopolitical Experience in Diverse Avocations as a Teacher, Physicist and Lawyer

From a Collection of Published Articles

T.R. COCA

Cover and interior design by the Book Cover Whisperer: ProfessionalBookCoverDesign.com

ISBN: 978-1-7345338-3-5 Paperback
ISBN: 978-1-7345338-4-2 eBook

Printed in the United States of America

FIRST EDITION

*This book is dedicated to my
beloved son, Dinesh C. Coca*

CONTENTS

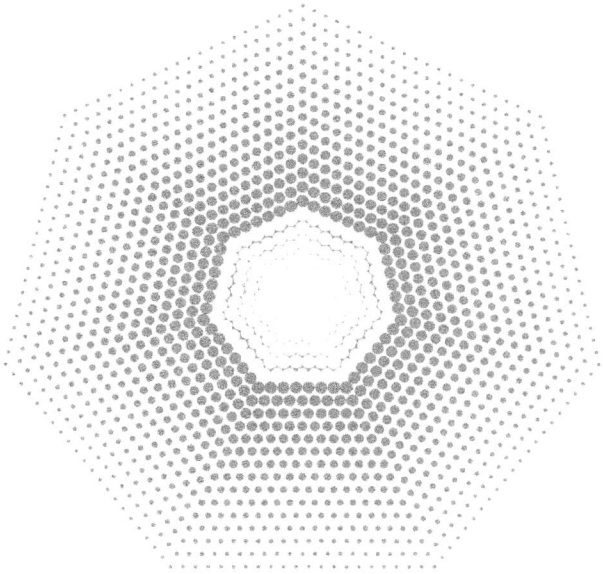

PREFACE

THIS BOOK IS A COLLECTION OF my writings which previously appeared in various forms and at various times in the local newspapers like the *Las Vegas Sun* and *Las Vegas Business Press* or as a post on the LinkedIn website. The writings are varied in content. They vary in length depending on the whims of the editors who published them.

I had a thrilling career as a physics teacher, physicist, Intellectual Property lawyer, licensor and litigator, mentor, advisor, and writer in the disciplines of physics and intellectual proper law. After writing dozens of papers in advanced physics and the specialty law of intellectual property, I took to general writing which this collection represents.

Part I of this book is a consolidation of thirty-one such writings which were published during the period of 2013-2020.

What connects my writings is the societal issue that was on my mind and in which I had some understanding and knowledge. Some issues were portrayed in the local news media as a burning topic of our society. The thread that connects my writings is a theme represented by the topics of Education, Innovation, Work, Immigration, Trade, China and America.

In Part II, I explain this connection. I also add my pragmatic advice to America which now stands at a crossroads.

These seven topics shaped the configuration of my writings, each representing a side and gave rise to the seven-sided polygon or heptagon. That is how "Heptagon Writings" became the title of my book.

When I selected a topic, I researched it, reached into my brain, identified an interesting issue, and applied my knowledge and career experience to pragmatically offer a solution for the readers to consider. My writings reflect the insights that I have which are relatable to others. They are like stories which needed a listener or a community of readership.

Each of my writings is an amalgamation of my critical analysis, serious contemplation, intellectual legacy and authorship. Other than this, no claim is made that my writings are comprehensive or scholarly. I intended my writing to be recreational reading. Read them casually. Use the advice I provide in my writings as down-to-earth if you chose to.

Otherwise, read for pure entertainment.

PART 1

WRITINGS

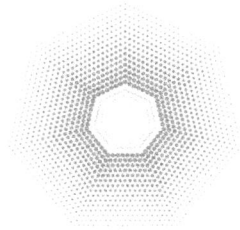

1

CAPITALIZE ON STATE UNIVERSITIES' ASSETS

Published in the Las Vegas Sun *on April 28, 2013*

WE ARE NOW A knowledge-based economy, and the ultimate engine of economic growth is new technology. The key drivers of technology are our universities and the researchers they employ, and today, perhaps more than ever, the products of the mind are humankind's most valuable assets.

Of course, it takes money to create new technology, and the universities depend on state and federal grants, which can be cut during tough budget times. However, there is a return on the public's investment in the form of new technology that can lead to new products and the underlying intellectual property. Because universities are not generally in the business of making goods, they are left with the IP assets, such as patents, and protecting those assets has never been more important to the universities.

In Nevada, University of Nevada, Las Vegas (UNLV) and University of Nevada, Reno (UNR) have developed a host of technologies over the years, including those in batteries, energy efficiency, renewable power, water efficiencies and mining techniques. Assuming that these public IP assets have been properly protected is our university system utilizing them to spur the Nevada economy?

That's an important question because university research should go hand-in-hand with economic development. The Nevada System of Higher Education should think like a business when it comes to the return on the investment. The return should not only be measured by the graduates it produces but also by the earnings it generates from the IP assets through leasing and selling the work its researchers do. Such earnings can be used to create new jobs, which Nevada badly needs, through commercialization of the IP assets. But it also can benefit academia by lowering the tuition costs to students, boosting faculty benefits to retain the best of the best and enhancing the academic stature. All of that is essential for a vibrant university system.

According to a survey of 157 universities by the Association of University Technology Managers, universities and their inventors earned more than $1.8 billion from commercializing their academic research in fiscal year 2011. Northwestern University earned the most of any institution, with more than $191 million in licensing income. Its revenue combined with four other $100 million-plus earners—the University of California system and Columbia, New York and Princeton universities—accounted for more than 40 percent of the total.

The universities used different models to harness their

IP assets, and together, the surveyed universities formed 617 start-ups.

The good universities are protective of the work their staff and faculty produces, as they should be, guiding inventors through the legal process to protect their work. Last December, Carnegie Mellon University enforced two of its semiconductor circuit patents against the chip maker Marvell Technology Group in federal court and won a preliminary judgment of $1.17 billion. At the final hearing on damages next month, the university is expected to ask for the award to be tripled, plus interest. The total award would be $3.8 billion.

That's the type of value a university can provide.

The Nevada System of Higher Education can learn from the highly successful universities to monetize the work its researchers do. The system and its universities should consider elevating their efforts to oversee intellectual assets. They should consider creating a high-level office dedicated to intellectual property that would aggressively work to capitalize on the universities' work. Such an office would be chartered with spurring invention through effective strategies, and that would include educating the research faculty and students about IP, harvesting their inventions, providing legal support and, more importantly, commercializing the IP assets.

Taking the IP and the underlying technology to market is like selling fresh fruit. IP is perishable, and new inventions and technologies have to be timely captured, protected and capitalized, lest they wither on the vine. To prevent that from happening, inventors should be given incentives to come forward with their work, and the universities should work urgently.

In this knowledge-based economy, a university must know how to timely deliver the IP and associated technology to the marketplace and facilitate its transformation into a tangible product by partnering with third parties. That provides lucrative licensing income for a university.

The Governor's Office of Economic Development is on the right track with its plans for the Knowledge Fund, which would provide money to help bring university research to market. This is the right way to bridge Nevada's highest priority of economic development and create jobs.

Still, roadblocks exist to commercialize university research and create jobs. An infrastructure is needed to help establish a viable push to oversee and market intellectual assets. A portion of the Knowledge Fund could be used to establish this infrastructure because it would be a great benefit to the state's economic development effort.

In a nutshell, what is important is a commitment to capitalize on the already created IP assets, timely harness new technologies that are being created in our university system and build new patent portfolio assets in order to sustain or grow job creation and economic development of Nevada.

2

FACULTY'S ROLE IN CONTROLLING TUITION

Published in the Las Vegas Sun *on April 19, 2014*

ARE UNIVERSITY FACULTY members doing their part to control the tuition costs that students are required to pay to pursue university education? Students are the reason for the existence of faculty in our colleges and universities. It is common knowledge that the tuition costs are steadily climbing at a higher clip than the rate of inflation.

Tuition and fees for taking 12 credits of course work at UNLV is $5,382 for a state resident. For nonresidents, tuition and fees mushroomed to $18,292. For graduate students, tuition and costs for residents and nonresidents for enrolling in nine credits of course work is $7,948 and $21,958, respectively.

Even at universities that are blessed with rich endowments such as Harvard, the University of Pennsylvania and Yale, there have been tuition increases this academic year in the range of 3 to 5 percent from the previous academic year.

As online education becomes more prevalent, the brick-and-mortar universities will face more pressure to increase their tuition costs because of a reduction in enrollment in such physical institutions. Compounding the higher cost of tuition is the uncertainty faced by students of finding suitable jobs after graduation. This has raised the question of whether there is a proper return on investment in a college education.

Given this, what can universities do to alleviate the burden of increasing tuition on students and their parents? More and more, universities are being asked to run as businesses. The bottom line is to generate a profit, as it will help alleviate runaway tuition increases.

It is the responsibility of not only the fundraisers at universities, but also the administrators, faculty and everyone else employed by the university to do their part to control tuition costs through innovation and efficiency.

Innovation is not reserved for those in white lab coats. There is room for innovation in the day-to-day processes that every employee carries out. For example, reducing the number of steps in an existing process can result in cost savings. It can also lead to efficiency of process. Both of these contribute to the bottom-line profit of the university.

Faculty members in particular bear a higher responsibility in not only controlling costs through the efficiency of process, but in actually raising cash for the university.

As a segment of the university population, the faculty salaries take a huge chunk of the budget. As universities vie for the best to serve on their faculty, this piece of the budget pie may not shrink unless measures are taken to enhance the revenue and profit of universities.

Participation in academic governance by faculty is central to the issue of alleviating the burden of increased tuition on students. Faculty members should reflect on how they can help alleviate the tuition problem. When they do, the answer become apparent: It is though monetization of faculty's intellectual abilities.

Universities should support and encourage faculty to offer guest lectures, seminars, and consulting, not to mention serving on the boards of outside organizations and writing books. The university could share some of the revenue faculty generate.

Scientific and engineering faculty members have a more direct way of monetizing their intellectual capabilities through commercialization activities. It is through obtaining rights for intellectual property in their inventions and commercially viable technology arising out of university research labs. The inventions made by the faculty make their way into patents with the help of the university legal department. These patents and other intellectual property would be owned by the university with a royalty sharing arrangement with the inventor.

Most universities do not actively monetize their innovative technologies, know-how and creative works often because universities do not have a requirement that the faculty generate revenue from these valuable assets. There is good reason for this. University research is funded to improve public health and promote open-ended scientific inquiry.

In addition, most university patents are not commercially applicable and remain unexploited. Also, the faculty tenure system at present is based on broadcasting knowledge and know-how, not contributing to commercial product development efforts. As a result, the vast majority of university intellectual property is distributed freely through scientific publications, through personal relationships with industry researchers and by graduating students out into the workforce.

Perhaps the faculty tenure process should be modified to make commercialization of intellectual capabilities a factor. Patents can be shared through license arrangements or outright sale. Likewise, know-how can be licensed with the faculty playing the role of facilitating the transfer of the technology from the research lab to the commercial establishment. Such activities generate ongoing or one-time royalties and can be structured to meet the revenue needs of the university and the responsible faculty.

Revenue generation for the university is now a universal activity of all faculty members. It should be made an integral part of the university statement of faculty's rights and responsibilities. Such activity is bound to ameliorate, if not reduce, a raise in student tuition.

3

HOW TO BRING JOBS BACK TO U.S.?

Published in Las Vegas Sun *on Aug. 3, 2014*

HISTORICALLY, UNEMPLOYMENT in the U.S. has been a short-term phenomenon. Most of the unemployed found work relatively quickly. However, as the Great Recession took hold, the level of unemployment rose to double digits; it since has dropped to 6.1 percent as of June.

Also, the quality of jobs created in the U.S. has deteriorated. Blue-collar jobs in manufacturing and white-collar jobs for highly skilled workers have been painfully slow to return.

The vast majority of job creation has been in the services industry. Manufacturing has been the backbone of the high standard of living in this country, but we have lost much of that industry.

There are two major reasons for the offshoring of U.S. jobs to foreign countries: free trade agreements coupled with a low wage structure offered by many foreign countries, and the U.S. corporate tax structure.

The U.S. is now a party to 14 free trade agreements. Notable among them are the 1985 North America Free Trade Agreement and the 2005 Central America Free Trade

Agreement. These agreements were intended to reduce tariffs, quotas and other trade restrictions among the signatories.

The U.S. aimed to promote the export of American products and expand the U.S. economy. For example, NAFTA made it easier for U.S. manufacturers to shift production facilities from the U.S. to Mexico to take advantage of low wages. This trend later shifted to China, with China's accession in 2001 to the World Trade Organization, as it offered lower wages, few workers' rights laws, a fixed currency pegged to the U.S. dollar, factories for new companies and few environmental regulations.

India, which also became a member of the WTO, benefited from the offshoring trend as it has a large pool of English-speaking people and technically proficient workers. India's offshoring industry took root in low-end software jobs in the early 1990s and since has moved to high-value-added jobs. Because of the talented pool of technical workers available in India and China, U.S. companies offshored even basic research-and-development jobs, which used to be reserved for U.S. workers.

However, the free trade agreements benefited the other countries much more than the U.S. The present high level of unemployment in the U.S. is attributed to offshoring. It is estimated that in the Great Recession, as many as 300,000 jobs per year have been offshored.

Initially, many U.S. companies were reluctant to move leading-edge technology needed for manufacture to China and India because of lax enforcement of intellectual property laws. However, these fears were sidetracked because of the low corporate taxes offered by the foreign countries.

U.S. corporate tax policies have an influence on offshoring U.S. jobs. The U.S. was the first nation in the world to implement a research-and-development tax credit in 1981. It now ranks 27th in the world in terms of tax incentive generosity. Also, U.S. corporations face the highest corporate tax in the world at 39.1 percent compared with Ireland at 12.5 percent, China at 20 percent, Poland at 19 percent and the U.K. at 23 percent. U.S. CEOs consider taxes as the top business threat.

U.S. corporations with global operations are allowed to defer taxes on their foreign profits. Under U.S. law, companies are not required to pay U.S. tax on their foreign subsidiaries' profits until the earnings are returned to the U.S. To avoid paying high taxes, many U.S. multinationals do not repatriate their foreign profits.

It may appear that the executives of U.S. corporations have no moral compass. However, by creation, corporations are capitalistic entities. The job of a corporate executive is to maximize profits to the shareholders.

The U.S. job market will not be healthy until changes are made to address the problems that affect our economy. The underlying problem is the lack of policies to incentivize U.S. businesses to create jobs in the U.S.

The U.S. should restore the research-and-development tax credit to reasonable levels in the 20 to 30 percent range, which would encourage businesses to invest in research and development in the U.S. as well as worker skill development. Going forward, the U.S. should lower the corporate tax rate to the low 20 percent range to be competitive with the rest of the developed world.

To motivate multinational companies to repatriate the money that they sheltered abroad, a one-time conditional tax holiday should be offered. The condition is that in return for repatriating the foreign profits tax-free, the companies should agree to reinvest that money to build the necessary research-and-development centers and manufacturing facilities, and create high-paying jobs in the U.S. combined with the necessary training in skills development to equip workers to handle such jobs.

With a judicious enactment as well as enforcement of such a policy, the jobs that moved offshore can be brought back to our shores.

4

WHY DOES U.S. GO TO WAR?

Published in the Las Vegas Sun *on October 5, 2014*

THE UNITED STATES just embarked on yet another war. This war is against the forces of the Islamic State who beheaded two U.S. journalists and are brutalizing countless innocent civilians in Iraq and Syria and attempting to take over these countries and impose strict Islamic law. We have been continuously at war since 2001 in Afghanistan and Iraq. Any war, particularly the modern war where sophisticated planes, unmanned drones, and cruise missiles carrying smart bombs are used, is extremely destructive on life and property. Wars drain our treasury. It is estimated that the wars we are in now are costing us the upwards of $100 million per day. Our military is tired after repeated deployments overseas. The American people are tired of war. Our allies who supported the American campaign in Afghanistan and Iraq are tired and have little to show for it. And yet, we embarked on a new war with a different set of allies supporting us.

Why are we perpetuating war?

We are a peace-loving nation. We would like to think that we enter just wars to preserve peace. As Theodore Roosevelt led us to believe, "a just war is in the long run is far better for man's soul than the most prosperous peace." In addition to preserving peace and prosperity, we go to war to preserve or expand other human values that we believe in. These are liberty, freedom of speech, human rights, and freedom to exercise one's religious beliefs without state intervention.

There was a period when we went to war reluctantly and only as a last resort. In fact we were forced into World War II when Japan attacked Pearl Harbor. Likewise, when the al Qaida terrorists attacked the World Trade Center and the Pentagon, we were compelled to pursue Osama Bin Laden and other al Qaida terrorists in Afghanistan which subsequently mushroomed into the wars in Afghanistan and Iraq.

We go to war because we believe that failure to act against aggressors would only invite further aggression. It is this belief that led us into Gulf War I in 1992 when we hastened to restore the small desert kingdom of Kuwait that has been invaded by its tyrant neighbor Iraq.

Some believe that the real reason we go to war is greed, weather it is money, oil or trade. They speculated that the second time we invaded Iraq it was not to dethrone the evil leader Saddam Hussain, but to control Iraq's vast oil reserves. However, history proved that we did not take advantage of Iraq's oil. In fact, we never take advantage of any country's resources, but only to liberate them.

Others believe that we go to war due to ego and fear. War allows our leaders to be powerful and us to feel safe and strong. It is this belief that made us confront the Russians

in a long Cold War after World War II until we succeeded and ultimately established ourselves as the world's sole
Superpower.

Underlying all of these noble reasons is the creation of the
military industrial complex composed of military contractors and lobbyists that perpetuate war. Dwight Eisenhower
warned us in 1961 that an immense military establishment
and a large arms industry have emerged as a hidden force in
America. It is this war-based economy that has addicted us
to what seems like a never ending war. In other words, we
do not endure war. We seem to need war for our economy
to thrive.

Military and Homeland Security budgets constitute one
of the highest components of the U.S. Government's annual
budget. The U.S. economy fueled by this vast budget creates
and sustains many jobs both in the government and civilian
sectors which support the war effort. In fact, when we are
at war, our economy based on the military and homeland
security seems to thrive. Investment in the shares of our
largest defense contractors has perennially yielded hand-
some returns because such establishments are the best in
developing and selling military weapons for huge profits.
We are the world's largest arm's dealer. We supply the latest
and greatest weapons to many of our key allies including
Israel, Saudi Arabia, and Taiwan and reap profits.

Although, we do not occupy other countries, except
during the time of war, our global military footprint is

pervasive. It is believed that we have over 660 military bases with active military operations in nearly 150 countries. The men and women in our all voluntary forces are gainfully employed by this vast military footprint and in the war-related activities in our country, while being prepared to sacrifice their lives. However, such war-based economy cannot sustain for too long as we are beginning to experience. The American people are wary of war and want peace and prosperity at home. And our treasury is depleted.

What we need is a complete overhaul of our economy. We should not be dependent on the economy fueled by the military industrial complex. We should stop feeding this beast. Instead, we should migrate to a totally civilian economy. What this requires is reversal of the prevailing investment by our businesses from creating jobs overseas to creating them in the U.S. This requires a correction of our mindset. Specifically, it requires a correction to our current corporate tax structure to incent profits that were already generated and sheltered overseas to repatriate those profits. Going forward lower our corporate tax rates to encourage businesses to create civilian jobs to rebuild and repair highways and bridges and other physical infrastructure in our country.

It would take a tough and resolute president and a patriotic Congress to reset our national priorities and resist the siren song for war abroad. The American people are ready and craving for such a reset.

5

U.S. LEADS IN TECHNOLOGY INNOVATION-DON'T LET OTHER COUNTRIES STEAL IT!

Published in the Las Vegas Sun *on November 5, 2014*

THE U.S. ECONOMY has undergone a major shift in the last 50 years. Because of our involvement in the Second World War, the U.S. established a preeminent industrial base. We essentially produced everything that the world wanted. By exporting our goods, our economy thrived, and our people collected high wages. This created a huge disparity in wages of workers relative to those in less developed countries. Being capitalists, U.S. businesses gradually shifted manufacturing to such low wage countries. This shift started with Japan and then moved on to Taiwan, Korea, Singapore, Malaysia and China to continuously take advantage of the falling labor rates. Because of this shift and transfer of associated U.S. technology, these Asian countries became rapidly industrialized.

Hardly a day goes by without doomsayers lamenting that everything we consume is now made in China. They cite our gridlocked political system, the deepening income and wealth inequalities and the growing clout of China and Russia as proof that America is on the decline.

The truth is that the U.S. migrated to a knowledge-based economy by relentless and continuous innovation. This migration has been accelerating at an incredible pace in the last two decades. The creation of the internet, the social media, new communication, transportation and e-commerce are the innovations that are the driving forces. Partly because the U.S. economy started out less regulated than others, so capital and labor can move more quickly, our innovation transformed into viable and more dynamic commercial enterprises.

Innovative uses of the internet and information technologies including effectively managing Big Data in the cloud storage, 3-D printing, and the growing communication between electronic devices (known as the Internet of Things) are poised to transform our industrial base. The automation and robotization of U.S. manufacturing plants are further increasing productivity, efficiency, and precision. As robotics capabilities increase, the cost of production of goods will decrease. The downside is that these machines are likely to displace many workers. Nevertheless, a reinvigorated U.S. economy is capable of putting a much larger portion of our population to work and keep unemployment low without risking wage inflation.

Adding to the innovation in technology, the U.S. is beginning to enjoy a boom in energy production. Fracking in which gas and oil are extracted from shale rocks by fracturing them is driving the energy boom. The resulting oil and the natural gas are lowering our energy costs.

Because of our innovation and lowered energy costs companies are already relocating their manufacturing operations from Asia to the U.S. to additionally benefit from savings in transportation costs and proximity to their U.S. research and design centers. Our industrial sectors are once again becoming the most competitive in the world. We had the strongest recovery of most developed countries and consumer sentiment, as measured by the University of Michigan, rose to 86.9 which is the highest since the Great Recession.

As our economy recovers, businesses need to be exceptionally cautious as other countries may face reduced demand for manufacturing upon which they thrived in the past. Importantly, technology transfer from the U.S. may slow down and these countries have fallen behind in innovation. This creates a perfect storm for them to catch up with the U.S. by taking the path of least resistance–by stealing our trade secrets.

What are trade secrets? We usually think of things like Coca-Cola's "secret formula", the recipe for the famous carbonated soft drink. However, trade secrets are much more. They are the fruits of our knowledge-based economy. Trade secrets presage all intellectual property and transform into patents, trademarks and copyrights upon taking certain legal measures. The confidential tools and systems built around corporate knowledge management are the modern face of trade secrets. For example, proprietary databases that capture credit-card data give a competitive advantage to the credit card company. Likewise, for an automobile manufacturer the confidential repository that captures the results of process improvement in production of automobiles is a powerful source of competitive advantage. Trade secrets are vulnerable. Once they are stolen, it can be incredibly difficult to stop their further dissemination and free use.

Laws to protect trade secrets exist in the U.S. at the state level (the Uniform Trades Secrets Act) and at the federal level (such as the Economic Espionage Act). They carry hefty civil and criminal penalties for violation. The Department of Justice has been intensifying industrial espionage of trade secrets by foreign countries. However, American companies have been lax when it comes to protecting trade secrets. Our open society and generosity based on trust to share our secrets with others may inadvertently turn us into philanthropists and rob us of our competitive commercial advantage, if appropriate steps are not taken. The first step is to place such secrets under a cyberlock with correctly configured firewalls—the equivalent of an unbreakable safe–and limit their access to authorized people.

Industrial espionage by foreign countries has reached a feverish stage. Cyber hacking by using sophisticated networks is the most favored weapon to steal our industrial secrets. Estimating the cost of cyber-espionage is tricky, but some economists estimate that the loss is as high as $120 billion annually.

Which countries are stealing our industrial secrets? According to the Director of FBI, China is the most active foreign power that is involved in the illegal acquisition of American industrial secrets. China has a massive and growing investment in its cyber espionage infrastructure and organization. In addition to using a vast network of agents, it recruits employees of U.S. companies to collect and steal our cutting-edge technologies and business intelligence. China places intense pressure on American companies to transfer technology to their Chinese partner companies under the guise of a joint venture as part of doing business in China. In order to remain globally competitive, the U.S. partners are almost always willing to provide technology and manufacturing expertise in order to obtain access to Chinese markets.

The operators behind China's espionage are the military often disguised as state-owned enterprises. Such SOEs are under intense pressure from their leaders to innovate and bring new technologies to the domestic market before the foreign firms can. However, China's record of genuine innovation remains paltry. Stealing information from U.S. companies is a cheaper and faster way to remedy innovation deficits and they have taken this path of least resistance. SOE's strategic sectors considered vital to China's future global leadership include energy and alternative fuel, bio- and nanotechnology, advanced manufacturing, high end materials such as rare earths and other emerging technologies.

China's stealing machine is not limited to commercial secrets. China, along with Russia, Iran and North Korea, are intruding our military establishment and government agencies to steal our military secrets and gain access to our national security intelligence. Last year's revelation by former NSA contractor Edward Snowden of our once-secret intelligence programs and the Wicky leaks earlier have been an unexpected boon to these foreign countries, while they dealt a blow to the U.S. Russia and China are now colluding after the West ratcheted up economic sanctions on Russia over the escalating Ukraine conflict.

As our economy moves to new heights, eternal vigilance to safeguard our innovation is imperative. In addition, our leaders should persuade Russia and China, the two most important points of resistance, to abide by a rule-based marketplace. The rule is simple: Thou Shall Not Steal!

6

U.S. IS A NATION WITH IMMIGRANTS

Published in my LinkedIn posts on December 22, 2014

IMMIGRATION TO THE U.S. is not a right. It is a privilege that is extended by the generosity of the American people. Many falsely utter that we are a nation of immigrants. This is false because out of the present U.S. population of 320 million, only about 40 million are naturalized citizens; include the 5 million that President Obama recently announced to grant amnesty and the legal immigrants, they together constitutes only about 12.5% of our population; include the illegal aliens of 12 million or so, all of this constitutes still only about 16%–17%.

Our natives were the American Indians and were born on American soil. The colonists from England and other parts of Europe who occupied our land and governed our natives constitute our Founders. The Founders encouraged immigration to America by offering substantial incentives, like subsidized land purchases, to meet America's labor needs.

The immigration issues were debated in the first Constitutional Convention. James Madison stated that *"America was indebted to immigration for her settlement and prosperity."*

Alexander Hamilton urged that immigrants be given equal status with other citizens.

Our immigration laws evolved over the centuries. Under our Constitution and rules set by the Congress, private employers, shipping companies and railroads and churches promoted immigration. Private companies recruited Chinese laborers to build our railroad system. The U.S. Army regularly recruited by offering immigration status to foreigners.

However, Americans were not totally comfortable with immigrants. Particularly after the 9/11 attacks, only 52% of Americans believed that immigration was a good thing overall for the U.S., down from 62% the year before according to a Gallop poll. They wanted controlled immigration based on the law and our national security and labor needs while continuing their generosity.

Historically, laws were passed to restrict immigration including the Chinese Exclusion Act of 1882 which blocked almost all immigration from China after the railroads were built. After World War I, Congress legislated the Emergency Quota Act followed by the Immigration Act of 1924 which lead up to the Immigration and Nationality Act of 1965 (INA). Under the INA and subsequent amendments, a complex national-origin quota system was established.

The quota system essentially eviscerated the historical goal to import the needed labor force and develop our country. Instead, family reunification of immigrants has taken the center stage. Now 66% of legal immigrants are admitted on this basis, along with 13% are admitted for their labor skills and 17% for humanitarian reasons. The latter is essentially derived from the kindness of American people to accord dignity to humanity who have been oppressed in foreign lands.

It is projected that if the present immigration policies were continued, the U.S. population will grow to 380 million by 2030 and to 600 million in about 60-70 years. The Census bureau projects that by 2050, one-quarter of the population will be of Hispanic origin.

Changes are needed to our immigration policy and the present quota system to meet the country's changed priorities. First, we should adjust the family reunification system which was founded on the concept of preserving the family unit of the immigrant. This unit has two components: the nuclear family and the extended immediate family. The nuclear family concept under which U.S. citizens can bring spouses, unmarried non-adult children and parents into the U.S. can continue as is. However, immigration of relatives of U.S. citizens such as married adult children, brothers and sisters should be curbed. This change is necessary, otherwise immigration of extended relatives, who in turn can bring their own extended relatives may cause a perpetual cycle of chain immigration.

The extended family unit concept is also outdated. Because of the vastness of our country, the family relatives after immigrating to the U.S. may not stay together as a unit in one place with the relative who sponsored them. Second, cheap and easy travel across borders coupled with improved communication renders the need for the family relatives to be co-located in the U.S. somewhat moot.

On the other hand, limiting immigration to the nuclear family may enhance quick assimilation of the migrated family into the U.S. society and accelerate the learning and use of English (by non-English speaking immigrants), which is essential for the unity of our country. In fact, the presence of the extended family may delay such assimilation.

Another change is that we should curb the present 17% of immigration on humanitarian grounds. While a reasonable number of refugees and asylees should be allowed to immigrate, the runaway mass amnesty, which appears to have been practiced by both the Republican and Democratic Presidents, should be ended. The solution to the influx of illegal aliens into America is better border control which is crucial for the national security and well-being of the American people.

Yet another change that is needed is that we should encourage immigration of foreign students who are receiving higher education, particularly in the science, technology, engineering, and math in our universities. We should allocate a much larger quota for permanent employment-based immigration and encourage foreigners with extraordinary ability in STEM, members of professions who hold other advanced degrees, persons with exceptional abilities, and skilled workers. We should enhance the temporary work visa programs for foreign workers who have the skills needed to start and run businesses with a promise to grant permanent immigration. In short, we should reverse the brain drain of our educated and revert to our original goal established by our Founders of inviting immigrants to meet our labor requirements.

7

THE ECONOMICS AND POLITICS OF OIL

Published on my LinkedIn posts on February 3, 2015

THE ECONOMICS OF OIL

The Organization of Petroleum Exporting Countries (OPEC) is composed of twelve members who include Kuwait, Iraq, Iran, Libya, Nigeria, Qatar, Saudi Arabia, Venezuela, and United Arab Emeritus. OPEC pumps about 40% of world's oil, with an output of 30 million barrels per day. Saudi Arabia is the largest oil producer in OPEC and wields an enormous power over oil production and establishes the price for its members.

The other oil producing countries, called the petro states, include Brazil, Canada, Columbia, Mexico and Russia. Their oil output is relatively small compared to that of OPEC. Over the last 2-3 years, the United States has joined the petro states as a significant supplier because of a combination of horizontal drilling and hydraulic fracking, which have unlocked supplies from shale formations including the Eagle Ford and Permian in Texas and the Bakken in North Dakota. The U.S. crude oil production now is over 9 million barrels per day. Because of this shale production, the U.S. has now reduced its importation of foreign oil and Saudi Arabia has been the oil producer who has been hit the hardest.

There has been a steep drop in the oil prices recently owing to the U.S. oil production. Contributing to this drop is the slowdown of the world's economic growth and higher efficiency of automobiles and other machinery that use oil as well as migration by some countries to alternative fuels. As a result, the international benchmark for oil has plunged by over 60% from the June 2014 peak. It is being speculated that oil could revisit the June 2008 low of $32 per barrel because OPEC, particularly Saudi Arabia, reiterated that it won't curb output to halt the price decline.

This drop in oil prices is far reaching on the world's economy. In general, those who are losing out the most are the countries who are net exporters of oil.

Among the OPEC countries, Venezuela and Iran are economically impacted harder than others. Venezuela is already in debt for tens of billions of dollars before the oil process dropped and heavily depends on its oil exports will suffer the most. Iran is most in trouble because of sanctions by the Western countries to arrest its quest for nuclear weapons which necessitated it to spend close to $100 billion last year alone on its consumer subsidies. The fighting that Iran is engaged in Iraq and Syria is further depleting its falling oil revenue. Saudi Arabia is able to weather the impact more than any other oil-exporting country because of its vast ($900 billion) cash holdings, mammoth oil reserves and its ability to produce oil at the cheapest rate than any other country. Saudi Arabia can break even with its oil production if the price of oil were to fall well below $30 per barrel. This is why it remains steadfast in letting prices fall.

Among the petro states, Russia is one of largest exporters of oil. While it has some cash reserves to guard against the loss of oil revenue, a combination of sanctions from the West imposed on it because of its involvement in the conflict in Ukraine and a falling ruble have made Russia even more dependent on oil.

On the other hand, the drop in oil price is a boon to many manufacturing and agricultural economies. China, India and Japan, which are major importers of oil, will significantly benefit and will continue manufacture and export of such goods without fear of inflation. Likewise, most agricultural counties which are dependent on oil for production of food will benefit.

Cheaper oil is bullish for the American economy on many fronts. If U.S. were to export oil, it will reduce our trade deficit and in, due course, may eliminate the huge debt obligation we face. Domestically, it reduces the cost of fuel for automobiles, trucks and airplanes and helps the American consumer. It widens the profit margins of our corporations who manufacturer goods and helps our farmers to grow feedstock and crops at a lower cost. The goods manufactured and feedstock and crops grown at a lower price will render them competitive for export which will further reduce out trade deficit.

THE POLITICS OF OIL

Over the last half a century, the U.S. and Saudi Arabia coop-erated with each other because the U.S. needed an assured supply of oil and the Saudi's needed the U.S. to protect and defend the kingdom's interests and ensure its stability in the chaotic Arab world. The U.S. established military bases on the Saudi soil and regularly trains its military personnel and supplies arms and the Saudi's ensure a free flow of oil. However, this is a handcuffed relationship and both counties are looking for ways to escape from the cuffs.

Saudi Arabia distrusts the U.S. now because of various events that took place recently. In Egypt, the Saudi's did not appreciate the help of U.S. to promote liberalism during the Arab Spring by easing Hosni Mubarak from power and the subsequent eagerness to approve the elected leader Moham-med Morsi of the Muslim Brotherhood who later attempted to promote a stricter version of Islam. Saudi's abhor the U.S. goal to reach a nuclear deal with Iran. They are baffled at U.S. tolerance to leave Syria's Bashar al-Assad in power as he slaughters Shiites and grows increasingly dependent on Iran.

The U.S. willingness to court Hamas allies Turkey and Qatar in the recent skirmish between Palestine and Israel is irksome to the Saudi's. They do not share the U.S. domestic values and reject the recent U.S. preaching against public

flogging and curtailing freedom for their women as interference in their internal matters.

Finally, the Saudi's have not gotten over the stigma that
all of the hijackers and the masterminds, including Osama
bin-Laden, behind the 9/11 attack against the U.S. were from
Saudi Arabia.

Saudi Arabia is playing politics with oil to control its
market share. Saudi's design is to let the oil prices drop to a
level that it makes impossible for the U.S. shale oil producers
to continue to increase their production and take some of
Saudi's market share.

More important, Saudi Arabia does not want Iran to
dominate in the Middle East which might happen if there
is a breakout in the ongoing nuclear talks with the U.S. and
the lifting of sanctions. By maintaining its market share and
ensuring low oil prices Saudi Arabia is determined to economically disrupt Iran from building the nuclear weapon.
An ancillary reason for the Saudi's to keep the oil process
low is to economically penalize Russia because it is an ally
of Iran and Syria.

This is an opportune time for the U.S. to wean out of its
dependence on the OPEC oil and the handcuffs of Saudi
Arabia by producing more shale oil. For the U.S. oil producers,
to continue or increase the present rate of oil production in
the face of falling prices will be economically painful. However, this pain could be ameliorated if our government can

pass sensible legislation to reduce taxes on such domestic oil production.

Additionally, the U.S. could enact legislation to build the Keystone XL pipeline to facilitate the export of oil. What is at stake is that the U.S. is now faced with a rare opportunity to take away the market share from OPEC and let the free market determine the price of oil. This will ultimately enable the U.S. to export oil, set our fiscal house in order and maintain our economic viability.

8

EUROPE'S INABILITY TO COMPETE WITH U. S. TECHNOLOGY

Published on June 25, 2015 in my LinkedIn postings

EUROPE AT ONE TIME was the model for innovation. Besides being the cradle of civilization, Europe reveled in the renaissance. The innovation that Europe drove in the fields such as astronomy, science, art, music and finance was once the envy of the world. The magnificent architectural wonders that survived centuries of time as well as the existing ruins bespeak of the charm and glory of this past innovation.

Although Europe earns its fair share of new patents, it struggles to turn these into viable commercial products. Europe's decline started with the World Wars. It has become acute in the last couple of decades when its commercialization of technological innovation stagnated and thereby set back its economy. Everyone knows that the European economy is now a mess.

The reason for the disparity between the technological success of the U. S. and the stagnation of Europe is the different models that the continents pursued combined with the lure of hard work and optimistic view of the Americans versus getting by with doing less work and eternal pessimism that engulfed the Europeans.

The U.S. has developed a unique model driven by its national security interest which uses more resources, takes higher risk and produces more revolutionary innovation. The key to the U.S. model is the absence of impenetrable barriers between various sectors involved in innovation such as between the public sector (including the defense establishment) and private sector as well as between establishments that are devoted to pure research and industry focused on product development. The U.S. government ensured public access to discoveries and encouraged free flow of information for sharing. This model contributed to the commercial development of nuclear power, the aerospace and semiconductor industries and ultimately to the Internet by spawning such iconic companies as Westinghouse, Boeing, Texas Instruments and IBM. Today, unlimited venture capital funding is additionally driving this model to new heights.

Venture capital investment in Europe lags behind the U.S. relative to the gross domestic product. The European model is based on rigid policies which do not promote entrepreneurial culture. The government imposes various taxes and red tape costs, long approval process, particularly for agriculture and biotech products, and stringent and costly testing requirements of new chemical substance for commercial use, which frustrate small businesses from commercializing technologies.

Look around Europe. Hardly any European giants now exists other than SAP (which, by the way, was founded by former employees of IBM) and Nokia, which is on the verge of extinction after Apple's successful commercialization of the iPhone.

Compounding the failed model that Europe has adopted, Europe has erected barriers against successful foreign companies who are doing business on the continent including IBM, Microsoft, Intel, and others. Under the guise of violating European anti-trust laws or not complying with standards established locally, Europe has fined and collected billions of dollars from these U.S. companies. Now Facebook, Google and Uber are facing similar barriers. The European Parliament is trying to thwart Google on the continent through restrictions in its search results. Likewise, Uber is coming under increasing pressure as taxi unions, with complicity from the government, combat the disruptive taxi service that Uber if offering.

The answer to European angst is not to erect barriers against successful foreign companies but evaluate its failed model for entrepreneurship. Perhaps Europe can collaborate with successful U.S. companies or emulate the U.S. model and try to regain its past renaissance.

Europe should also develop an entrepreneurial culture by embarking on sound economic policies with tax breaks, less red tape and gentle support for nascent businesses struggling to establish on its soil. Most of all, Europe should establish role models of successful entrepreneurs for other Europeans to look up and emulate them.

9

WHAT IS EXPECTED FROM AN IN-HOUSE INTELLECTUAL PROPERTY ATTORNEY?

Published in the Las Vegas Business Press *on August 1, 2016*

TODAY, TECHNOLOGICAL INNOVATION drives almost everything. Creation, protection, and exploitation of new ideas are paramount for organizations to survive, whether the organization is driven by hardware, software or services. Particularly when new ideas are created, patent and trademark protection is conventional. Over and above, in case of organizations engaged in software, advocating a way for its copyright and trade secret protection need to be achieved. One should be adept not only in the protection of software whether it is offered as a service or stored in the cloud, but also facilitate its exploitation for profit.

Innovation without protection and exploitation of the fruits of innovation is nothing other than practicing philanthropy with any organization's R&D investment. The investment strategy should be designed to find a sustainable competitive edge by focusing on the organization's IP as the top priority. The value attributed to a company's IP far exceeds its physical, employee and other assets and could be longer lasting if properly used.

Key to this strategy is a well-rounded and experienced in-house IP attorney. The attorney should create a tailored IP strategy and leverage it.

The first step is cultivating a culture of knowledge of the IP in the organization. The attorney should actively engage with internal business leaders and product design and development teams in the organization, conduct IP training, such as unique "invention harvesting sessions" for engineers by conversing in their technical jargon, and document their ideas. Managing the submitted inventions, having them evaluated by in-house technical and business development experts, and obtaining patent protection by engaging external patent lawyers follow. Likewise, when software is created, the in-house IP attorney should establish an unobtrusive way for its copyright protection (including tamper-proofing of the marketed code by applying the Digital Millennium Copyright Act) and/or trade secret protection. Develop a SUPER (select-use-protect-enforce-renew) methodology to protect the distinctive styles and colors (also known as brands or trademarks) in which your product is marketed, and messaging is communicated. Managing this virtuous cycle of IP creation, protection and exploitation is imperative for the organization's success.

Astute planning and developing a global IP portfolio for your organization to ensure freedom to operate and bestow a competitive defensive advantage comes next. Not all technology and IP can be created in-house to meet your organization's needs. The in-house attorney should assess such needs and facilitate purchase or license-in the necessary IP to satisfy them. Appropriately divesting unneeded IP and generate income is an option that should be exercised, as called for.

Actively directing and managing relationship with U.S. and foreign outside counsels for worldwide patent prosecution as well as litigation should be second nature to the in-house IP attorney. Quality patent filing and prosecution requires inscrutable attention to detail. Patents are often the most valuable asset. The downside is they are expensive to pursue and maintain. The attorney should design a tiered approach to patents by ascribing a value rating to the patent and intimately link the filing, prosecution and maintenance costs to the rating. By this approach, more high quality patents are procured and maintained for a longer duration. Second, the in-house attorney should furnish written guidelines to the outside prosecution counsels and administer them to ameliorate their run-away billing costs.

Likewise, in patent litigation, whether before the federal courts or the International Trade Commission, the in-house attorney should be capable of devising practical strategies, actively engage with the litigators to review correspondence and legal arguments and can direct briefs in support of litigation. Minimizing exorbitant litigation expenses while always keeping the door open for level-headed settlements is crucial.

The in-house attorney should have a proven ability to license patents and technology to 3rd parties. Patent licensing is an art which requires tenacity, patience, perseverance and courage. Precise reading of your organization's validated patent claims on the infringing product is the needed proof. Engaging with the infringer, sharing such proof and negotiating with persistence will eventually lead to an outbound license.

Any unused technology developed by your organization is an asset that the in-house attorney should capitalize on to cultivate partnerships and/or generate income. This requires building a technology roadmap, establishing the nexus between your company's technology and patents, finding a suitable partner who can commercialize it, negotiating and structuring a deal and facilitating the technology transfer.

The in-house professional should be proficient in applying legal analysis in strategic transactions with 3rd parties and assist in problem-solving, no matter how complex they are. What is important is a judicious balance of the risk and reward in transactions and exercising it.

Establishing a structured framework to implement IP strategies with written policies, practices and guidelines is a vital part for the success of the IP function. Prepare such document repositories and systematically implement and administer them. Such written policies would lay a strong foundation for the IP strategy and deliver consistent and sound results predicated on ethical IP practice.

10

CORPORATIONS HAVE LEGAL, ETHICAL AND ECONOMIC RESPONSIBILITIES

Published in the Las Vegas Business Press *on December 4, 2016*

WITH THE ELECTION of Donald Trump as our next president, American companies are destined to face a major shakeup in their corporate governance. Mr. Trump's campaign promise of reducing the U.S. taxes that corporations are required to pay to 15 percent from 35 percent and granting a tax break to repatriate the trillions of dollars of profit earned from overseas sales and housed in kinder jurisdictions to avoid U.S. taxes, seem to be preordained. This is an opportunity for U.S. corporations to modify their corporate governance to meet changing demands for their success and for the good of the country in which they are incorporated and do business.

Foremost in corporate governance is a re-examination of whether they are being good corporate citizens. If not, they should quickly adapt toward achieving this all-important goal.

Corporations are governed by the basic principle of a fiduciary duty as established by the stockholders. The fiduciary duty includes legal, ethical and economic responsibilities.

Overlapping these is the unwritten duty of corporate citizenship, which involves social and community responsibilities. In other words, citizenship is a commitment to be socially accountable for the impact they make on the community of the country where they are incorporated.

The first step to good corporate citizenship is generating profit while practicing the established legal and ethical principles. Labor costs figure prominently for companies that produce goods. Over the last several decades they were lured to shift production to countries where the labor costs were low. This practice met their economic goal.

A hidden fact of engaging a foreign entity in producing products is that the American company is compelled to disclose its manufacturing technology. This entails teaching the foreign entity the recipe (known as the "know-how" and "show-how," in legal parlance) needed to manufacture. Such recipe is generally not protected by patents but held within the company as a highly prized trade secret. This technology transfer is intended solely to make the product for the benefit of the American company. However, in reality, despite the existence of contracts under which the recipe is disclosed, the foreign entities, particularly those based in China, are known to breach those contracts. Worse, after learning from the American company how to make the product, the foreign entities develop a competing product and go into business for themselves, thereby undercutting the profit for the American company.

Given this reality, American companies before outsourcing their production should carefully weigh the benefit of cheap labor versus the cost of losing the technology shared with the foreign entity. The latter is far more economically valuable and provides a lasting competitive advantage than the cost savings realized from cheap labor.

Compounding this, the American companies pay a mounting social price when they outsource jobs that were once held by their U.S. employees. Actually, such job elimination enraged the U.S. workers and played a large role in the election of Trump, who promised to bring such jobs back to our shores.

Will President Trump be able to bring back millions of jobs? It depends on the cooperation of U.S. corporations and their moral compass to step on the path to be good corporate citizens.

Due to the great number of potential workers in China, India, Vietnam and other up-and-coming lands, there remains a worldwide excess of labor that will continue to keep a downward pressure on labor costs. What should a company that produces goods to do under these circumstances?

A trade-off should be achieved to balance the competing interest between profit and creating jobs for Americans. The U.S. companies should continue to take advantage of low-labor costs available overseas, but they should weigh this economic gain against their citizenship responsibility.

They should offshore only repetitive, low-end, labor-intensive and essentially "robotized" manufacturing and assembly jobs. High-paying jobs, which require technical skills such as those associated with design and development of innovative products, should be reserved for U.S. workers. The design and development are the most important phase of a product life cycle. In this phase, creative juices flow and new intellectual property is created.

Such intellectual property is probably the single most valuable corporate asset. It should be harnessed for economic gain by seeking worldwide legal protection and safeguarded, as needed, by keeping it in-house under lock and key.

Next, it is the duty of the American companies to provide the necessary training to the U.S. workforce in the new skills that are needed to design and develop innovative products and equip them for today's digital factories. With the cost savings they realized by the reduction of corporate taxes, this is an opportune time for companies to invest in such training.

The United States has essentially become a knowledge-based economy. For decades, our companies took pride in creating cutting-edge products by making huge investments in research labs and development centers in the country. The fruits of this creativity, in addition to producing and selling new products and generating profit, were protected as intellectual property (patents, trademarks, copyrights and trade secrets). By licensing such intellectual property the companies derived additional and longer-lasting economic benefit.

When our corporations shifted their R&D centers overseas, they inadvertently created a sieve in the protection of
their new intellectual property. Most countries including
China, India and Vietnam do not offer the same infrastructure to be creative as what is available in the U.S., and the
protection of intellectual property in those countries is not
as advanced as here. Second, these foreign workers are not as
loyal as U.S. employees to safeguard the intellectual property.
As a result, the value of this intellectual asset is significantly
diminished and the return on the investment made in establishing R&D centers abroad has been lessened.

As labor cost in foreign countries rise, outsourcing of
U.S. jobs will shrink. Already companies are beginning to
see that it is now no more expensive to hire U.S. workers in
states such as Alabama, Nevada, Mississippi, and Tennes-
see to produce goods. This factor combined with the cost of
transportation of the finished goods from the foreign country
to the U.S. and the long time and resources needed to oversee the production pace and quality of the finished product
should further motivate American companies to reverse
their course to outsource jobs. Many state governments are
eager to have jobs created in their state by offering special
tax incentives and other concessions in return. Companies
should avail of these incentives as they fulfill not only their
economic duty but also their social responsibility.

An overt display of good corporate citizenship can
burnish the public image and enhance the sales of the

company's products. Socially responsible investment funds enjoy a higher return to shareholders because certain kind of social responsibility associated with nationalism and patriotism is bound to pay off.

Shareholders and corporate officers have an important role to play now. Just like we expect individual American citizens to show patriotism and loyalty to our country, the shareholders and officers should take the corporate bull by the horns and put the company they own on the path to meet its corporate citizenship responsibilities as an indispensable part of the fiduciary duty.

11

SMALL BUSINESSES MUST PROTECT INTELLECTUAL PROPERTY

Published in the Las Vegas Business Press *on March 13, 2017*

IN OUR PRESENT knowledge-based economy, small business owners have a tradition of creating innovative products and good jobs and opening new sectors of the American marketplace. "Invent or die" is the motto under which small, innovative, high-tech businesses operate. The most precious asset for such business owners is the newly minted intellectual property that launched their business.

Many owners, however, might lack the knowledge and expertise necessary to prevent the theft of their innovation. Or else, the owners ignore it as they see images of expensive lawyers and distraction of their precious time which competes with raising the needed capital for their new business.

For small innovative companies, the ability to grow and prosper requires more than luck. It hinges upon securing IP protection for their innovation.

Copyright protection does not require a lawyer. Likewise, domestic trademark, trade dress and domain name protections can be achieved relatively cheaply without the aid of a lawyer. To obtain patent protection, however, requires a patent agent or attorney and can be costly.

The U.S. government encourages domestic small business entities to seek patents by offering lower fees for filing and prosecution in the U.S. Patent &Trademark Office. In addition, the USPTO enables them to explore their technological potential and provides incentives to profit from its commercialization.

"Patent or perish" should be the motto of small business entities that are engaged, especially, in high-tech. This does not mean that every idea that comes out of the business needs to be patented. Start with an internal discussion of what ideas have been protected, if the new idea is protectable, and if it is important to your core business.

IP protection and its strategy should be part of the on-going business plan. Such strategy is vital to securing the financing and investments needed to build and scale the business. Investors view the IP portfolio as an asset and distinguish your business from the others who lack it.

Patents, when properly shepherded through the system, could be the most prized possession of any business. Downstream, they can be used to prevent a competitor from making, using or selling your patented technology without your permission. They can be used to generate income if your business opts to license. Also, your patents could serve as trading material for a cross-license arrangement with others if your own business were to infringe on their patents.

On the other hand, if your business does not wish to share your patented technology with a third party, you should be able to enforce your rights. Patent enforcement, however, is the sport of kings! You need to engage a patent litigation firm. The average cost associated with litigation of a single patent in the U.S. courts is now about $3.5 million. Even after winning, there is no guarantee that a court will grant a permanent injunction against the losing party. You might be asked to settle for money damages and extend a license for a fee.

Many small business owners do not seem to understand that patents (as well as trademarks, trade dress and domain names) are territorial in nature. In other words, even if your business has protected these IP assets in the U.S., they are not automatically protected in other countries. As a result, the small business must develop an international IP strategy to obtain protection in a selected number of foreign countries where your product is most likely to be manufactured or sold.

A lot of the choice comes down to what your business plan calls for. Your business should consult an IP expert and conduct a cost-benefit analysis to see if expanding your IP rights makes sense. Small businesses that export their IP to other countries where it is not locally protected might face rampant theft without any recourse. Even if a small business were to engage a foreign-based manufacturer to build a prototype of the product, motivated by taking advantage of lower overseas labor costs or to investigate the product's feasibility, it has the potential for theft even if contractual agreements are put in place, as such agreements are generally difficult to enforce in many countries.

It is critical for an innovative business to take steps to safeguard its IP to hone a competitive advantage. Such protection discourages theft by competitors. It provides you the business incentive to commercialize the IP and profit from it.

Legal protection of IP tends to be expensive, particularly in the early phases of the business development cycle when the financial capital is sparse. IP protection is also time sensitive. If it is not protected in a timely manner, it might perish. Despite these pressures, it is well worth the initial investment of time and money. The rewards derived from such asset protection will last for a long time–until well after the expiration of such rights.

12

DIVERSITY + INCLUSION = INNOVATION

Published in the Las Vegas Business Press *on May 1, 2017*

INNOVATION IS FRESH thinking that leads to valuable products and services. Innovation is not limited to invention that generally is visualized as made by people in white lab coats with a high IQ. Innovation is a special culture that businesses cultivate. It is a culture of creation. Central to the innovation culture in our present connected world is diversity, inclusion and a work environment which fosters creative thinking.

People exposed to diverse backgrounds and imbued with the spirit of teaming will produce an unexpected solution to a problem. They tend to analyze the problem differently and through brainstorming will come up with a blend, leading to a brand-new idea.

Innovation starts with curiosity–a burning desire to experiment and explore new things that contribute to success in what we do. It requires passion to pull together one's strength and energy toward success. The willingness to take a chance early on while addressing a problem is what leads to innovation. More important, innovation requires relationship building or teaming. Teaming provides a moral and intellectual platform that allows one to connect, organize, accelerate and succeed. Sometimes cross-pollination in a team environment is potent to create entirely new ways to innovate, particularly if the members have a diverse cultural and educational background.

Tesla Motors is classic example of cross pollination of people having diverse educational backgrounds. Rather than starting his automobile company siloed in Detroit, Elan Musk founded it in the heart of Silicon Valley where cross pollination of ideas from the information technology, mobile communications, artificial intelligence and robotics are integrated to innovate a new, versatile and desirable electric car.

Innovation has no boundaries. It can happen in almost every aspect of business. For example, reducing unnecessary steps in a routine process to achieve the end result is innovation; as such reduction could make the process more efficient, reduce waste and save costs. In fact, such a new process with reduced number of process steps is considered as an invention that can be patented.

Today the common complaint is too much information. The trick is not to get bogged down in details but harness the patterns behind the information and apply them in a meaningful way to build new products and services that makes life better. That is true innovation.

Innovation happens all around us. It sometime seems obvious. When you see innovation, you wonder "why didn't I think of it?"

13

REFORM OF U.S. IMMIGRATION LAWS IS NEEDED

Published in the Las Vegas Business Press *on July 17, 2017*

WHILE CONSIDERABLE ATTENTION is being given to the millions of foreigners who unlawfully entered the U.S. in the recent past, there are serious flaws in our immigration laws that allow lawful immigration. Some of the flaws include the H1-B and EB-5 visa programs, limited quota placed on professionals holding advanced degrees, and the undue breadth of family-sponsored immigration, all of which could lead to an eventual green card (lawful permanent residency). There is a dire need to reform the U.S. immigration law to fix these and other existing flaws.

H1-B VISA: STEM IMMIGRANT

This visa allows U.S. employers to temporarily hire foreign workers who have graduate-level education in occupations that require expertise in fields like science, technology, engineering, math (STEM), finance, accounting, medicine, etc. Each year a total of 85,000 visas are granted and they are widely used primarily by employers based in the Silicon Valley. These employers tend to pay H1-B workers $65,000 to $75,000 a year, far less than the $100,000 or more for U.S.

workers. Nearly 70 percent of all H1-B visas go to workers from India.

The H1-B visa was originally intended to be a non-immigrant visa, initially granted for up to three years but many extend it to a maximum of six years and then apply for the green card. The H1-B visa holder can bring their spouse and children less than 21 years of age to the U.S. as dependents under the H-4 visa category. An H-4 visa holder is not eligible to work in the U.S., but they find ways to circumvent this restriction and take U.S. jobs for reduced wages.

U.S. employers like Microsoft, Facebook and Cisco openly and regularly canvass our executive and legislative branches to bolster the H1-B visa program by shedding crocodile tears that they cannot find skilled American workers. The fact of the matter is that these employers are not seriously looking to find the skilled American workers. One reason is that the online job-seeking platforms they use are inherently impersonal and flawed in their functionality. Even if the American worker who was found in the job search is not a complete match for the open position, they would become a fitting match with some on-the-job training.

Unfortunately, many U.S. employers are unwilling to invest in American workers by providing on-the-job training as the H1-B visa holders are an easy way to meet their hiring needs. They use the H1-B visa holders to depress wages for American workers as the imported workers are willing to work for less. Such employers have no other motive than corporate greed to enhance their profits. They lack the moral and social responsibility of a good corporate citizen. One way of reforming the U.S. employers disregard to retrain the American workers to meet their job requirements is to suspend or ditch the H1-B visa program altogether.

EB-5 VISA: IMMIGRANT INVESTOR

Under this visa program a non-US national can apply for a green card by investing as little as $500,000 in a business in an economically disadvantaged area and be actively engaged with it by creating at least 10 full-time jobs. The investment should remain in the business for at least three years and produce a service or product that benefits the U.S. economy. The EB-5 visa holder will be able to bring their spouse and unmarried children under the age of 21 and can get green cards for all of them.

Green cards for EB-5 investors are limited to 10,000 per year. Accompanying relatives (which, on average, is two family members per investor) are not counted in this limit. Chinese investors are the vast majority of the applicants using this program. According to the State Department 9,128 of the EB-5 visas were allocated to the Chinese investors in 2016. The next biggest number of 225 went to the South Korean nationals.

For wealthy foreigners, the EB-5 program is the fastest, cheapest and best bet for getting the green card. Because of the ease of getting an EB-5 visa, there are currently 22,000 applicants in the backlog. However, scandals of visas going to people with criminal records, investors receiving green cards without actually creating very many jobs and swindlers defrauding potential investors have been in the news. This has been known to be a scandal-ridden visa program.

Some reform is underway in Congress for the EB-5 visa program to increase the investment amount to $1.3 million. However, this investment is still too small. It should be increased to $5 million. The lifetime value that can be attributed to each green card procured under the EB-5 program will exceed tens of millions of dollars. Importantly, what is needed is strict federal anti-fraud measures and tight oversight.

EMPLOYMENT-BASED (EB) VISA

U.S. Immigration laws have certain numerical limits on the number of immigrants admitted by category each year, the total limit being 675,000. These limits, however, are not simple numbers. They are calculated based on rather complicated formula. The annual quota of visas allocated to employment-based category is 140,000, which include the quota for EB-5 visa. The employment-based visa is designed for foreigners holding professions with advanced degrees, persons of exceptional ability, skilled workers and other professionals. Reform is needed to bolster this quota to 300,000.

Every year American universities graduate 300,000 foreign students with STEM degrees. These students have already received valuable education and have the potential to be entrepreneurs and skilled workers. The immigration laws should be reformed to encourage opportunities for these graduates to apply for green card and remain in the U.S. These graduates will readily fill the void created by the proposed elimination of the H1-B program.

FAMILY-SPONSORED VISA
Foreigners who earned a green card are allowed to sponsor immediate relatives, including their spouse, unmarried children who are under 21 years of age; and U.S. citizens who previously held a green card can sponsor parents, brothers and sisters. The concept behind this family sponsorship is to preserve the unity of the family in the U.S. The assigned quota for a green card to brothers and sisters is 65,000. This category of sponsorship should be eliminated.

The concept of family unity is outdated. Even if the sponsored brother or sister were to receive the green card, the possibility of the brother or sister living in the same geography in the U.S. as the sponsor is limited. Second, in our interconnected world, it makes little difference whether the brother or sister is physically present in the U.S. or in the foreign country where they now live.

In summary, the U.S. immigration laws are based on meeting the country's economic and security needs. We imported foreign workers and generously harbored them when our country needed them. The times have changed. We now need to create jobs for Americans and regain the strength and economic vitality of our nation. While the suggested changes may look somewhat self-centered, they are needed in the best interest of our country, now.

14

INNOVATION: A SPECIAL CULTURE THAT BUSINESSES CULTIVATE

Published in the Las Vegas Business Press *on May 21, 2017*

INNOVATION IS FRESH thinking that leads to valuable products and services. Innovation is not limited to inventing. That generally is visualized as made by people in white lab coats with a high IQ. Innovation is a special culture that businesses cultivate. It is a culture of creation. Central to the innovation culture in our present connected world is diversity, inclusion and a work environment which fosters creative thinking.

People exposed to diverse backgrounds and imbued with the spirit of teaming will produce an unexpected solution to a problem. They tend to analyze the problem differently and through brainstorming will come up with a blend, leading to a brand-new idea.

Innovation starts with curiosity—a burning desire to experiment and explore new things that contribute to success in what we do. It requires passion to pull together one's strength and energy toward success. The willingness to take a chance early on while addressing a problem is what leads to innovation. More importantly, innovation requires relationship building or teaming. Teaming provides a moral and intellectual platform that allows one to connect, organize, accelerate and succeed. Sometimes, cross-pollination in a team environment is potent to create entirely new ways to innovate, particularly if the members have a diverse cultural and educational background.

Tesla Motors is a classic example of cross-pollination of people having diverse educational backgrounds. Rather than starting his automobile company siloed in Detroit, Elan Musk founded it in the heart of Silicon Valley where cross-pollination of ideas from information technology, mobile communications, artificial intelligence and robotics are integrated to innovate a new, versatile and desirable electric car.

Innovation has no boundaries. It can happen in almost every aspect of business. For example, reducing unnecessary steps in a routine process to achieve the end result is innovation; as such reduction could make the process more efficient, reduce waste and save costs. In fact, such a new process with a reduced number of steps is considered an invention that can be patented.

Today, the common complaint is too much information. The trick is not to get bogged down in details but harness the patterns behind the information and apply them in a meaningful way to build new products and services that make life better. That is true innovation.

Innovation happens all around us. It sometimes seems obvious. When you see innovation, you wonder "why didn't I think of it?"

15

ALLOW IMMIGRANTS WHO SATISFY U.S. LABOR NEEDS

FROM OUR COLONIAL days, immigration was encouraged to meet America's labor needs. The present national-origin quota system undermines the goal to import the labor needed. Instead, family reunification of immigrants has taken the center stage. Now 66% of immigrants are admitted on this basis, 13% are admitted for their labor skills and 17% for humanitarian reasons.

The family reunification system founded on the concept of preserving the immigrant's family unit needs to be changed. This system is composed of the nuclear family and the extended family. The nuclear family, under which citizens can bring spouses, unmarried non-adult children and parents into the U.S., should continue. However, immigration of other relatives of citizens should be curbed. If not curbed, the extended family will continue to bring their extended relatives, and this will cause a perpetual cycle of chain immigration.

The extended family unit concept is outdated. Because of job mobility, the relatives after immigrating to the U.S. do not stay as a unit near the relative who sponsored them.

Easy travel between countries and improved communication renders the need for co-location of the extended family moot.

Limiting immigration to the nuclear family will accelerate assimilation of the migrated family into the U.S. society which is essential for the unity of our country.

Another needed change is to end the runaway mass amnesty. The solution to the influx of illegal aliens into America is better border control which is crucial for the security of the U.S.

Finally, encourage immigration of foreign students who are receiving higher education in our universities. We should allocate a larger quota to foreigners with advanced degrees, exceptional abilities and needed skills for immigration. We should revert to our goal of inviting immigrants to meet our labor requirements.

16

A WORLD WITHOUT AMERICA

Published on July 30, 2017 as my LinkedIn post

JOHN MCCAIN THE veteran senator in a floor speech before the U.S. Senate on July 26, 2017 said that America "is a nation conceived in liberty and dedicated to the proposition that all men are created equal. More people have lived free and prosperous lives here than in any other nation. We have acquired unprecedented wealth and power because of our governing principles…."

"America has made a greater contribution than any other nation to an international order that has liberated more people from tyranny and poverty than ever before in history. We have been the greatest example, the greatest supporter and the greatest defender of that order. We aren't afraid. We don't covet other people's land and wealth. We don't hide behind walls. We breach them. We are a blessing to humanity."

American has given so much to the world and so often without expecting anything in return except the desire to promote democracy and our governing principles. Every year we contribute over $30 billion to the budgets of world organizations to promote peace and harmony through dialog. We donate hundreds of billions of dollars in foreign aid to mitigate starvation and decease across the world. We voluntarily expend our wealth and sacrifice and shed the blood of our citizens by waging wars against rogue nations to bring about justice. We rebuild the destroyed nations after such wars like we did in Germany and Japan and make them prosper.

It is unfathomable to imagine a world without America. However, if America were suddenly ceased to exist, what will the new world be like?

New spheres of influence will be established. Human rights, free speech and liberty, the essential elements of American democracy, will take a back seat. The Earth's environment will take a hit. There will be less international order, more misery, chaos and tension.

The existing spheres of influence and the balance of control that comes from it will be upset. Absent the U.S., Russia and China will emerge as the new superpowers that carve up the new world to dramatically expand their spheres of influence. Russia will expand its sphere to the European continent that it does not already control. It will expand to the Middle East and exert control of the oil resources in that region. Russia will accelerate its ocean navigation in the Arctic Circle linking the Atlantic to the Pacific Ocean and exert its sphere of influence over Canada and what used to be the U.S. and spread its tentacles to Mexico, the Caribbean, Central America and South America. In effect, both poles of the earth will be under Russia's orbit of influence.

China will gobble up Taiwan immediately. It will annex the Korean peninsula on the pretext of avoiding a preemptive nuclear strike by North Korea against its southern neighbor.

China will expand its sphere of influence to the entire Asian continent including as far down as India, South Pacific including Australia, New Zealand, and other island nations in that region. China will expand its sphere to Africa where it is already present and exploiting natural resources such as minerals in some African countries. China will continue this exploitation without just compensation. Racial discrimination in Africa will get worse. In the Indian subcontinent China will suppress the Indian people out of fear for their superior human intellect in an effort to minimize competition.

With the world divided up this way between the former communists, democracy will be crushed everywhere. Freedom of speech and religion will be a memory, particularly to the previous democratic nations. Human compassion and sympathy which America championed and promoted, especially when natural and man-made disasters struck anywhere in the world by rushing aid in the form of food, medicine, equipment, and human services will take a hit.

Human ingenuity and innovation which America spearheaded will suffer. Without the U.S., Russia and China will have no place to commit espionage to steal new ideas, technology and trade secrets. Lacking new ideas, technological progress will stagnate in the new world.

World treaties like the World Trade Organization, the

North American Free Trade Agreement and judicial bodies like the World Court, defense establishments like the North Atlantic Treaty Organization and forums like the United Nations Organization will demise as will the cooperation between the remaining dominant powers. In fact, these powers will be at each other's throat and make the people in their orbit miserable by forcing them to conform to their perceived world order.

There will a total disregard for the earth's environment. The two domineering powers will pay scant regard to the carbon emissions and other pollutants which hollow out the earth's ozone layer and contribute to the rising of the oceans. The melting of the ice in the Arctic will be a boon to Russia for easier navigation and control of the Arctic. Russian and China will be blinded by ambition to dominate the other at any cost, even at the peril of the earth's environment.

The new world's economy will implode because of excessive forced regulation on regional monetary policies, absence of free enterprise and control over trade between counties that violate the superpower's perceived world order to dominate.

In general, the new world will be a dark place devoid of the stability and order that the present world is accustomed to. Regional wars will break out without the U.S. serving as a world's cop to maintain law and order. India and Pakistan at the slightest provocation will unleash their nuclear weapons with scant regard for China's influence killing hundreds of millions of their people. The other bitter enemies Iran and Israel will unleash their nuclear might at each other to their mutual destruction. Russia will be helpless in such a conflict despite its expected sphere of influence in the Middle East.

America is not perfect. Yet, the ennobling principles upon which American is founded and our continued desire to follow them makes it the best country for any human being would aspire to live in. Our magnanimity has been boundless. Partly because of this we seem to have lost our edge over the wealth that we earned through hard work and dedication to our principles. However, that loss is temporary. We are bound to regain that edge, reestablish our power and remake America great once again! Importantly, we will continue to relentlessly serve the world.

Is it too much to ask the world to acknowledge our contribution to humanity and emulate us?

17

MULTILATERAL VS. BILATERAL TRADE AGREEMENT: WHICH IS BETTER FOR U.S. ECONOMY?

Published in the in Las Vegas Business Press *on January 2, 2018*

THE *Wall Street Journal* recently commented that Europe and Japan finalized the trans-Pacific partnership (TPP) trade pact that eliminates tariffs on more than 95 percent of products and reduces non-tariff barriers. It commented that the U.S. lost by walking away from the TPP.

After becoming president, Donald Trump withdrew from the TPP which was between the U.S. and 11 other countries bordering the Pacific Ocean. He promised to replace it with an agreement negotiated on a bilateral basis.

Let us analyze whether a bilateral or multilateral trade agreement would serve the U.S. interests better?

MULTILATERAL AGREEMENT

Multilateral trade agreements are treaties of commerce between three or more nations. All signatories treat each other the same. The treaties are intended to confer such benefits as reduce tariffs and make it easier for participating countries to import and export products, give expanded access to each other's markets and increase each country's economic growth. These agreements standardize business operations and commerce regulations; establish fair labor standards and environmental protection. The goals are to keep one signatory country from stealing the other's intellectual property, dumping products at a cheap cost, or using unfair subsidies. Since multilateral deals level the playing field for all signatories, it is particularly beneficial for emerging market economies which are smaller in size and less competitive.

The biggest disadvantage of multilateral agreements is that they are complex. The details of the negotiation are specific to trade and business practices. That means the public often misunderstands them. Consequently, they receive lots of controversy and protests. Another disadvantage is that since trade barriers disappear smaller businesses cannot compete with giant multinationals. They often lay off workers to cut costs. Others move their businesses to a participant country where the wages are low.

That makes multilateral deals unpopular. Multilateral agreements are difficult to enforce. Another issue with multilateral deals is that other countries gang up on the U.S. and force demands that are detrimental to the U.S.

Examples abound of multilateral deals that the U.S. signed: Besides the TPP, the North American Free Trade Agreement (NAFTA) signed in 1994 between the U.S., Canada and Mexico, the Central American Free Trade Agreement (CAFTA) signed in 2004 by the U.S. with Costa Rica,

Dominican Republic, Guatemala, Honduras, Nicaragua and El Salvador, the 1947 GATT (General Tariff on Trade and Tariff) agreement which paved the way to the WTO (World Trade Organization) agreement among all 149 member countries. Besides these, agreements specific to intellectual property, which is a key part of all trade deals, have been signed such as the Paris Convention for patents, the Universal Copyright Convention and the Berne Convention for copyrights, and the trade agreement among the members of the World Trade Organization (WTO), to name a few.

BILATERAL AGREEMENT

Bilateral agreements are between two nations at a time, giving them favored trading status with each other. The objectives of the bilateral deal are the same as a multilateral deal, except it is between two countries that negotiated the deal.

The advantages of a bilateral agreement is that it is easier to negotiate since it involves only two countries; goes into effect faster, reaping trade benefits more quickly. They are easier to enforce, particularly if arbitration is the specified means to resolve a dispute.

Examples of bilateral agreements: The Transatlantic Trade Investment Partnership (TTIP) agreement between the U.S. and the European Union, which has been stalled in negotiation following Brinton's decision to exit the EU. The TTIP is intended not only as an economic project, but also a political project to promote transatlantic ties. This would be the largest agreement so far, beating NAFTA.

The U.S. has entered into bilateral deals with 12 other countries. These countries and the year the deal went into effect are: Australia (2005), Bahrain (2006), Chile (2004), Columbia (2011), Israel (1985), Jordan, Korea (2012), Morocco (2006), Oman (2009), Panama (2011), Peru (2009), and Singapore (2004).

ANALYSIS

All of the dozen bilateral deals had great impact on reducing tariffs, increasing U.S. exports, providing protection for intellectual property and increasing effective labor standards and environmental enforcement. None of these deals face unsolvable disputes of violation of the signed deal.

The multilateral treaties were intended to provide increased trade. However, they failed to fully bestow the trade benefits that the U.S. expected. Because of NAFTA, many U.S. manufacturing jobs went to Mexico hollowing out many industrial states the year after NAFTA went into effect.

The various treaties on intellectual property and the WTO deal are totally ineffective. This may explain President Trump's flip from being a supporter of multilateral treaties to bilateral deals. China is the primary violator of the WTO and intellectual property agreements. In the first 15 years of accession to WTO only China achieved one-sided win outcome rather than a win-win with the U.S. and the rest of the world.

First, U.S. inventions which are protected by patents here are not likewise protected in China. Even if protected by patents in China, they are difficult to enforce against Chinese infringers. The reason is that Chinese businesses systematically engage in copying U.S. products and undercut the American economy.

China has not been living up to its obligations under the IP treaties it signed. Moreover, China has been aggressively driving espionage to steal U.S. intellectual property by overtly engaging its military and other state organizations.

China is known to dump on our soil, goods such as steel, solar panels, toys, pharmaceutical products, etc. made with generous state subsidies in violation of the WTO deal.

A trick that China pulled off before acceding to WTO is that it used coalitional bargaining to define its status as a developing country and unfairly conferred certain benefits on itself. China has ample capacity to wage a trade war against any major economic power like the U.S. and EU. It exploited its incorrect status as a developing country to a significant extent. China failed to adopt a proactive opening up strategy by acknowledging that it is a developed country and play by the required rules.

CONCLUSION

The pros and cons of multilateral and bilateral agreements do not seem to favor one type over the other. However, it is unclear that without the U.S. participation and leadership as a chief advocate what fate multilateral deals will face and whether globalization will continue. This is an interesting experiment awaiting results.

President Trump's strategy to recuse the U.S. from participating in multilateral deals should be allowed to run its course until this experiment is completed. Trump may be proven to be right that a more-controlled trade by the U.S. via bilateral deals will lead U.S. to greater strength and prosperity. Certainly, his trade policy is jolting us out of a profound amnesia and complacency into fresh thought and action.

Regardless, our country should maintain its open economy and leverage its market power to strengthen it by creating more jobs. The U.S. should establish a standardized template for bilateral agreements and institutionalize such template for reaching deals with all countries. Such template may become the gold standard for all countries.

18

TRADE TARIFFS VERSUS U.S. JOBS

Published in the Las Vegas Business Press *on March 26, 2018*

FOLLOWING PRESIDENT DONALD Trump's recent announcement to impose trade tariffs on imported steel and aluminum a lot has been written and spoken in the media against such a move. Most of it was negative, falsely creating gloom and doom scenarios and improperly labelling it as a protectionist measure.

Clearly, Trump's measured action on tariffs is not protectionist. It is aimed at rebuilding the American economy by bringing back U.S. jobs that we held, and which were lost by unfair competition and flagrant violation of existing trade agreements by our trading partners. Trump's action is in concert with our free economy, but it uses the leverage of our market power to set right such violations.

The U.S. pioneered a culture of innovation. Innovation does not grow on trees. It takes a concerted effort to create, promote and nurture innovation. By establishing an educational infrastructure to foster human intellect and supporting its gestation by passing laws that promote free enterprise; and providing economic stability free of red tape, our government facilitates to harness our innovation to create high-paying jobs and build successful enterprises. Our innovation is the envy of the world. Many foreign countries constantly steal our innovation even though it is protected by worldwide intellectual property rights.

About three decades ago, we started losing our jobs for many reasons including:

1. The push by our government to sign free-trade agreements with foreign partners, such as the North America Free Trade Agreement, the World Trade Organization Agreement, Central America Free Trade Agreement, etc.
2. High U.S. corporate tax structure that was imposed on our companies, which discouraged them to repatriate the profits that they made overseas.
3. Cheap labor that became available overseas, which our companies took advantage of to have goods made overseas.

In part, because of the trade agreements that U. S. signed, our consumer seemed happy because the prices of goods went down.

However, the cheap consumer goods came at a heavy price. Many U.S. companies were too eager to do business overseas, particularly with China because of its low labor costs and perceived scale of opportunity to sell our products in that country. Our companies shared their valuable technology with ventures set up in China owned jointly by the American company and a Chinese partner, with the expectation that the Chinese venture partner would produce goods at a lower price than in the U.S. However, after the technology was transferred and goods were successfully produced, many of the ventures were deliberately terminated by the Chinese partner and the latter went into business on their own by using the U.S. technology and undercut the American companies.

Another destructive effect was the American entity shut down its U.S. manufacturing base and permanently destroyed jobs that were held by our workers since it relied on the Chinese partner to produce goods. The myopic view of the U.S. companies to trust the Chinese partners and transfer their precious intellectual property and depend on them to produce goods backfired. Because of this misguided practice, Chinese imitators of the U.S. companies came into existence. Examples of the American company and their Chinese copycat companies abound: Cisco—Huawei; Apple—Xiomi; Google—Baidu; Amazon–Alibaba; EBay–Taobao; and Priceline–Ctrip, etc.

President Trump made an election promise in 2016 to bring such lost jobs back to the U.S. He has been steadfast in fulfilling that promise. With his signing of the tax bill in December 2017, which reduces federal corporate taxes and incentives to repatriate over a trillion and half dollars parked overseas, he took the first steps to keep that promise. The tax cut is a boon to everyone—rich and poor. It makes our companies reinvest their profits to create high-paying U.S jobs.

Because of the tax holiday followed by a repurchase of shares by our companies, the value of their share price has been rising. This is good because the pension funds on which the retirement benefits of many U.S. workers depend are thriving, thereby reassuring a potential good return.

The president's trade announcement is fully in concert with his approach to further fulfill his promise to bring back jobs. As an opening salvo, it puts on notice all countries that have not been trading with our country on a fair and equitable footing. Countries, which have violated the trade agreements and unreasonably dumped goods, such as automobiles, solar panels, basic steel and aluminum, washing machines and garments, on our soil should realize that such dumping resulted in destroying our industries and precipitated the loss of millions of jobs. But for this unfair trade practice by foreign partners, U.S. jobs would have not been lost.

Some fear the affected foreign violators will retaliate by imposing reciprocal tariffs on U.S. exports. This is to be expected. However, such retaliation will be suicidal.

The U.S. is blessed with an enormous leverage when it comes to trading with other countries. Our economy is so huge that every foreign country is eager to sell their goods to us. With the newly enacted tax structure, the U.S. will continue to be an even stronger and more stable economy. With the anticipated boost of the U.S. dollar received from a successful handling of trade on fair terms, we will buttress the U.S. dollar as a reserve currency for the world to continue to rely on. The U.S. economic engine is bound to regain its strength and will pull the economies of the world that depend on it. We will soon be a net exporter of oil and natural gas. If a trading partner does not wish to renegotiate the trade deficit that U.S. is facing, it is free to decouple from this engine, but it will be left off and will lose immensely.

Many countries conduct trade on fair terms with us, but some want free trade, not fair trade. Notable among them is China. Trump's new trade policy is aimed primarily at China.

Recent newspaper reports accuse China of being the main culprit in stealing our technology, know-how and intellectual property, as well as hollowing out our industries of jobs. In addition, national media have reported that China planted its state-sponsored agents posing as legitimate employees in our national labs and private entities to steal technology through espionage. Trump should confront Chinese officials against these activities and impose all permissible trade sanctions to arrest such activities.

President Trump is a disruptor. In our modern corporate world disruptors are prized. Trump does not believe in maintaining status-quo. He is bold and a risk-taker which is what the U.S. needs now. We have long been afraid of change and resigned to a status-quo no matter how ineffective it has been to our economy, our governing principles and the welfare of our people, particularly in providing our people with meaningful work. The president should change the U.S. jobs landscape by using trade as a weapon to bring them back to our shores. What is needed is a set of targeted tariffs on the goods imported from China. If he succeeds, it will be one of his best accomplishments and the nation will be grateful.

19

NEVADA MUST EDUCATE MORE STEM GRADS FAST

Published in the Las Vegas Business Press *on April 24, 2018*

THERE IS GROWING optimism that Nevada's economy is on the mend. The business environment indicates strong promise of growth over the next several years. Part of the reason for this optimism is the federal tax law that was enacted in December 2017, which dramatically reduced the corporate tax on profits and encouraged multinational corporations, which sheltered abroad profits earned overseas, to repatriate those profits. Our tax system is now competitive with other nations and our companies would now remain under U.S. ownership and those businesses that moved overseas may return to our shores.

In short, the benefits of our new tax code will create robust demand for jobs in our country. The reduced federal regulation of our businesses is adding confidence that they can compete in world economy.

In addition, partly because of the 2017 federal tax reform that curtailed certain deductions from wages, and primarily because of the sky-rocketing real estate prices and high state income tax structure in states like California, both individuals and corporations from California are beginning to migrate to Nevada. This is an opportune time for Nevada to rise up to the needs of this movement.

The educational system in Nevada traditionally produced more low-skilled workers suited for our service industry. With the anticipated workers needed for businesses that are knowledge- and skill-based, our education system needs to produce industrious and technologically skilled workers to meet this demand.

It is well-known that graduates from Nevada high schools, when they enter college, need remedial training and supplementary coursework. More important, our students are not acquiring skills in science (physics, chemistry, biology, etc.), technology, engineering and math (STEM) in proportion to the jobs that business are seeking to fill. This is a double whammy of poor quality and inadequate quantity of STEM grads that Nevada education system is producing.

Moreover, females are underrepresented in some STEM skills in quantitative fields like physics, chemistry and engineering and computer science with notable exception (like biology, nursing science, zoology, pharmacy and veterinary medicine). This under representation is a disadvantage to employers who want to promote gender equality in careers and also enhance the benefits of diversity of their professionals. One way to remedy this problem is for guidance counselors and parents of middle and high school girls to encourage them to pursue STEM subjects.

The types of professional careers of the future that

businesses are looking to fill are varied: software coders; electricians; communication specialists; battery technologists; solar power plant construction and maintenance workers; biologists who have the ability to harness big data in medicine and in managing patients in hospitals; engineers who can design products and services using artificial intelligence; skilled talent in biotechnology, information technology, health care, autonomous-driving vehicle technology; drones for aerial photography; aerial inspection of deep-sea oil rigs and delivery of packages; robotics, including designing robots to handle industrial jobs, such as automobile manufacture; intelligent robots to manage inventory in industrial warehouses; military robots to deliver weapons in the battle field and to fight wars; and police robots to control crime in urban centers.

The Nevada system of higher education faces a dual challenge. First, it should impart STEM skills to our students that match the needs of our businesses. Second, it has a very short window of opportunity to accomplish this, as the businesses hiring needs are immediate and cannot wait indefinitely. This requires re-engineering and innovation in how education is delivered in Nevada.

The best approach to meet these demands is this: Create a crash education program leading to an associate degree, diploma or apprentice in STEM requiring one to two years (preferably, one calendar year) after secondary education. Such a program should be administered by Nevada's existing two-year colleges. The focus of these colleges should be a singular and concentrated skill development in STEM.

Our colleges should impart computational prowess to solve problems by encouraging creativity in students. Our businesses have a responsibility to our colleges in providing this education, too. Prospective employers should participate in the development of skills they require by loaning their talented employees to train the enrolled students. These employers should also incent the enrolled students with paid on-the-job internships (for example, during the summer months) and promise to hire students after graduation from the STEM program. Such cooperation between our educational system and employers is vital to make the program successful.

This will be a win-win for the Nevada's higher education system and the employers, as it will bring the two perspectives together by meeting the employers' skill demand with the system's goal to impart and accelerate the right career-training vocational technical programs in technology have been highly successful in industrialized countries like Germany, China and India. These countries decades ago realized the value of training in STEM and heavily invested in meeting such need for their citizenry. They immensely profited from such investment.

The return on investment in attending the traditional four-year college is diminishing in the U.S. It has been reported that tuition costs alone exceed more than $100,000 to earn a four-year degree from Nevada's colleges. Studies also indicate that it takes decades to recoup such investment particularly from non-STEM careers. The skills that a majority of our four-year degree programs are creating are not commensurate with the jobs that our economy is demanding. It is time to wake up to this reality and redirect Nevada's education system and align it with proper STEM education and skill development of our graduating students to fully meet the needs of our economy.

20

BOOMERS' SKILLS, EXPERIENCE ARE TERRIBLE THINGS TO WASTE

Published in the Las Vegas Business Press *on June 19, 2018*

THE U.S. UNEMPLOYMENT rate is at a historical low. Our businesses are seeking skilled workers, which our higher education system is unable to produce to meet their demand. Some employers are clamoring to increase importation of foreign workers through HB-1 and EB-5 visa programs, which the federal government is attempting to curb. However, the employers seem to be overlooking a huge available pool of talent and experience that exists in our midst right now. This is the pool of baby boomers.

According to Pew Research Center, there are reportedly 75 million baby boomers born between 1946 and 1964, which represent a third of our population. The boomers are highly educated (more than 29 percent of boomers have a bachelor's or higher degree), highly experienced and the wealthiest population group. They tend to be former mid-level and high-level managers and qualified in science, engineering, technology, and precision manufacturing trades. They received formal training and possess a tremendous amount of intellectual capital such as know-how, which can be earned only through years of on-the-job experience. In short, the baby boomers are the muscle of our industry. The retirement of baby boomers will continue to create skill shortage and certain industries are going to be hit hard.

The boomers seek self-control over their lives. They cherish the freedom and ability to live independently but want to remain social and have meaningful connections with the society. One of their needs is to be able to contribute their knowledge and skills to the next generation by either volunteering their services or continuing to productively work at their leisurely pace without the pressure or grind of work. Their desire to work is not so much based on the need to accumulate more wealth, but to genuinely mentor the next generation of workers.

The baby boomers are a source of tremendous talent. They gained professional skills and experience across the job spectrum starting from architects to zoologists. Harnessing their skills and experience and accommodating them to meet the critical shortage that our country is facing is something that our employers seem to have overlooked or deliberately ignored. As a result, a generation of valuable talent is not being captured. Some boomers are volunteering their services to established religious and educational organizations and to others such as SCORE (Service Core of Retired Executives). In fact, it is reported that the boomers have the highest volunteer rate of any age group. Despite this high participation, the number of volunteer hours is not sufficiently high or sustained to fully capture their talent and experience. Often, there is a mismatch between the boomers' skills and the volunteering tasks they are performing, which renders the skill transfer not fully satisfying to the boomer.

A better and pragmatic approach for capturing the boomers' talent and experience is for businesses to seek them out and hire them as contract employees either part time or full time, depending on their mutual needs. By hiring as a contract employee, the boomers health care needs, vacation and retirement benefits do not take the center stage and they lessen the economic burden on the employer. Such an approach will be a win-win for both. The employer recruits a valuable and highly trained worker, who can immediately mentor and transfer experience to another hired rookie employee in the business without the fully loaded burden of hiring a regular employee. The boomer receives the satisfaction of enabling the next generation employee with professional development by imparting the knowledge and skills he earned over his lifetime.

The society at large receives a side benefit by this approach. First, the valuable talent and experience of the boomer is not let go to waste. Second, by continuing to be gainfully employed, the boomer can put off collecting the entitled social security benefits until mandated by the age requirement, which will be a reprieve for our already stressed Social Security system.

Professional recruiting agencies are ineffective to identify boomers having specific skill and talent set as these agencies are generally trained to develop a tunnel vision based solely on age and myopically focus on the younger millennials, despite the existence of age-discrimination laws, and seldom look at resume' of older and experienced boomers. The best way to target boomer talent is to specifically seek in job advertisements for experienced applicants having specified talent for hire on a contract-based and flexible position. Another source is to approach an organization, such as SCORE, which is known to have in their certified business mentor directory retired executives possessing many talents. SCORE operates throughout the U.S. and has thousands of retired executives to choose from. Additional sources include the Coming of Age and the Senior Job Bank.

The baby boomers are a highly prized intellectual asset of the U.S. We should take advantage of their invaluable skill and talent particularly at this juncture where there is a dire need for utilization of such an asset. We should not let this precious national asset go to waste.

21

RUNNING FOR ELECTION OF BOARD OF REGENTS IN NEVADA

Published on July 30, 2018 as my LinkedIn post

I AM EXTREMELY interested in politics. I am fascinated by what has been happening in politics in the last fifty-three years in the United Sates. I never ran for office until I decided in March 2018 to run for the position of University Board of Regents, District 12 in Nevada.

To understand what motivated my run for the regent's position I need to dwell into my background, the large number of years I devoted to gain broad education and deep professional experience encompassing many careers. Let me dwell on my past after which I will return to my story on the candidacy for the regent.

Who am I?

Having been born in India and spent my early childhood there, I developed a disdain for politicians because of the rampant corruption in the election process that takes place there. The two professions I detested were politicians and lawyers. I thought they were the scum of the earth and they ended up in those professions in India as a last resort because they failed in everything else.

I came to the U.S. with the aspiration to be a physicist. Having earned at an early age my Bachelor's degree in physics and math and a Master's in nuclear physics from the University of Mysore (which now changed its name to Karnataka University), I was lucky to have qualified for graduate school admission coupled with a teaching assistant ship at Temple University. The admission and assistantship paved the way for my entry into the U.S. under a student visa.

As required, I taught laboratory physics to undergrads at Temple while taking graduate level course in physics on the side. I earned a second master's degree this time in optical physics. Then, my study for Ph. D in the field of solid-state physics followed.

While many of my classmates in grad school were Americans, there were a few foreign students from mainland China, Taiwan, Korea and India. The foreign students especially from China were brilliant and ferociously competitive. Because of this intense competition, it was quite stressful to maintain a cumulative grade point average of 3.0 or higher. Nevertheless, the bell curve that my professors employed for grading the class placed the foreign students' grades at the leading edge of the curve. Because of this shift some of my American classmates were disadvantaged and they worried that their cumulative grade point average may fall below the mandated minimum or else they may be drafted into the military and get dispatched to the war in Vietnam. A few of them decided to voluntarily take jobs in the military establishments such as the Sandia lab.

I dedicated to my studies as if nothing else mattered and completed my course work with good grades. In about four years I passed the Ph.D. preliminary examination.

Because the U.S. wanted to retain foreign students who were pursuing advanced degrees in technology, the Immigration & Naturalization Service offered a special preference to such students to convert their temporary student visa to permanent visa (known as the Green Card) status. I applied for and quickly earned my Green Card, which gave me the green light to apply for any job in the country, including government jobs which required the top-secret security clearance.

What remained to be completed in my Ph.D. program was to conduct research on an approved topic and write my thesis. I got carried away by ambition to be famous from my scientific work. With encouragement from my thesis advisor, I embarked on a mission to discover a high temperature superconducting material. Such discovery would have been a milestone in human ingenuity and would have revolutionized the energy industry. However, after six months of intense concoction of various alloys involving lead, indium, niobium, and thallium and testing the critical temperature at which the alloys exhibited superconducting properties, it became frustratingly clear that I was on an unrealistic track.

Pragmatism prevailed and I settled for the realistic research topic of understanding the magnetic hysteresis of the alloy that I concocted. Eighteen months later, I completed and successfully defended my thesis. I could then add the prefix of "Doctor" to my name!

However, when I graduated with my doctorate, lady luck did not smile on me! Initially, I craved to work in research labs of IBM or AT&T since the physicists there were attempting to find the elusive high temperature superconductor like I did, but the doors there were shut. I sent hundreds of job inquiries to other employers. I even tried to buy time by working as a post-doctoral fellow in the university, but no such luck.

A political happening caused an unexpected job shortage even for the brightest. I was caught up in President's Nixon's political maneuver to end the war in Vietnam and get reelected. The U.S. House of Representatives reduced the defense budget to end the war in Vietnam. As a result, thousands of engineers and scientists were laid off from jobs in the defense and related industries. In fact, many such laid-off workers were reported to be driving taxi cabs in cities in California, New York and Texas. A fresh graduate like me did not stand a chance to compete with this unexpected glut of talent.

I settled for teaching advanced physics at the Abington High in suburban Philadelphia in order to make a living and to be close to my Ph.D. thesis advisor. There remained an unfinished task with my thesis. I needed to publish papers in journals based on it. Such papers were an important credential on a scientists' resume. "Publish or perish" was the accepted motto for scientists then, as it is now. With help from my advisor, I was able to publish half a dozen papers in prestigious journals.

While teaching I took additional courses in education for the mandated Pennsylvania State certification as an Instructor, I availed of the opportunities in the evening to teach more physics at the Montgomery County Community College and Weidner College. Within a short period I earned my Instructor certification and tenure at Abington, but continued to be driven by goals to go beyond the comfortable life on college campus.

While I knew that sooner or later I will find a job as a physicist, I opted to take a courageous risk for opening a new window of career opportunity. I decided to pursue the study of law in the evening law school at Temple while continuing to teach. My objective was to synergistically marry my technology background with law to become an Intellectual Property attorney. In as much as I disdained the law profession when I lived in India, l was fascinated by how our Founding fathers wrote a fresh and thoughtful U.S. Constitution from which statutes, rules and regulations derived and they enabled an orderly operation of the country.

Two years into the 4-year J.D. program, I jumped at a wonderful job opportunity at the defense contractor General Dynamics Corporation in San Diego, CA as a Senior Research Engineer. I jumped for two reasons: it offered the path to work as a physicist that I was trained for; and it enabled me to pursue my J.D. course study without interruption at the University of San Diego Law School in the evening.

As anticipated, even before I graduated, I received lucrative job offers from law firms and companies. One such offer was from the Patent Department of NCR Corp in Dayton, OH which I grabbed as it enabled me to be closer to my wife who was pursuing her residency in medicine in the neighboring state of Missouri. The next challenge was to meet NCR's requirement to be admitted to two Bars: the State Bar of Ohio, and the Patent Bar of the United States Patent & Trademark Office.

Studying for and taking the bar examination is a grueling task. It requires dedication, discipline and concentration to thoroughly understand all aspects of federal and state laws as well as human patience, perseverance and stamina to take the examination. After taking hundreds of hours of bar review courses and rehearsal of practice tests, I passed the Ohio bar examination on my first try.

Next was passing the specialty patent bar exam which is conducted by the United States Patent and Trademark Office on patent statutes, rules, regulations, and practice procedures. The pass rate in this exam when I took it was low: 25-30%. Having passed it, I thought I earned a reprieve and can focus on my family, but such reprieve was short lived.

I changed my job as a corporate patent attorney to IBM, which was a New York company and encouraged its attorneys who aspired to climb the management ladder to be admitted to the local bar. I had management aspiration. Accordingly, I recharged myself and accomplished all that was needed to be done and earned my bar membership in New York which opened up a horizon for my professional advancement in IBM. My life at IBM has been a thrilling run.

Many brilliant people worked in IBM including mathematicians, physicists, chemists, computer scientist to name a few specialties. A few were the Nobel Prize winners. They carved new frontiers in their fields of study bringing fame and fortune to themselves, to IBM and to USA. The inventions they made were simply mind boggling. To understand the scientific breakthroughs the researchers achieved required superior scientific knowledge. This is where my strong background in optical, nuclear and solid-state physics came handy. In my capacity as a patent attorney I could speak their language, make intelligent conversation, and genuinely applaud their brilliance and the technical breakthroughs they made. Importantly, my synergistic combination of physics and law rendered easy to document their ideas for legal protection.

It seemed ironic that a decade earlier, fresh after earning my Ph.D. I dreamed of working at IBM. That avenue was not open for me then. However, by taking a new path I made my way into IBM in a different capacity—as a coveted patent professional. Also, the aspiration that I had of finding the elusive high temperature superconductor for my doctoral dissertation a decade earlier actually was realized in 1986 by my fellow scientists who worked in the IBM Research Labs in Zurich for which they deservedly won the Nobel Prize in Physics that year.

Even though I had the luxury of a dedicated client, namely the employees of IBM, I had to simultaneously keep multiple balls in the air to fulfill my job responsibilities: stay on top of the semiconductor technology to understand the cutting-edge inventions of my client; keep abreast of the federal, state and local laws in order to provide the right legal advice; and be intimately linked to my practice in Intellectual Property law, which meant a complete and up-to-date knowledge of patents, copyrights, trademarks, trade secrets, the semiconductor chip protection law and more. These demanded endless hours of reading technical, legal and IP literature day after day on my own time. Writing patent applications, documents such as responses, petitions, appeal briefs associated with patent prosecution and handling transactions kept me productively occupied.

Being a glutton for punishment, I took interest in a brand-new law known as the U.S. Semiconductor Protection Act that was just passed by the U.S. Congress and signed by the President. I boldly took the pioneering task of registering valuable IBM semiconductor chips for mask work protection in the U.S. Copyright Office under the new law. All of this effort culminated in my contributing a comprehensive chapter on "Chip Protection, Licensing, Litigation and

International Issues" to a five-volume legal treatise *Intellectual Property Litigation & Licensing.*

The next twenty years brought a whirlwind of professional and personal growth which will take a book to narrate. I will limit this story to major milestones. I was promoted to Patent Counsel and moved to IBM's facilities in Burlington, VT, where I had the complete responsibility to manage a 15 person IP department and counsel a group of 12,000 IBM employees. As you guessed it, IBM expected that I earn membership in Vermont's Bar, which I did. While I was barely settling into this job, when IBM offered me a plum job, which attorneys crave for and wait for a lifetime. I was asked to head to Tokyo to be the Chief IP Counsel for the Asia-Pacific region.

Being known to raise my hand for new opportunities, I accepted and unceremoniously plucked my family and moved to Tokyo for this international assignment. A new set of experiences and monumental challenges involving new workers, new cultures, new languages and new sets of international laws were waiting for me.

The new job called for handling multifarious responsibilities which broadly were: supervise a 75 person team, manage the foreign IP portfolio, license and enforces IBM IP rights. I supervised the teams dispersed in Australia, China, Hong Kong, Japan, South Korea, and Taiwan by studying, learning and adapting to the cultural differences of people and differences in laws on IP protection and enforcement.

Based on the culture, I tailored a slow and patient pace with my teams in China and Japan and regularly coached them on the best practices of IP protection. In China, I demonstrated hands-on involvement in drafting and negotiating joint venture agreements. I accelerated my pace with the teams in Australia, Hong Kong, South Korea, and Taiwan, because they were more communicative and developed better English language skills, and coached them for patent and trademark protection and enforcement in their respective countries. By holding annual team gatherings in Tokyo, I established a strong sense of collaboration and a bond of common purpose among them under the IBM principles and practices.

An enduring leadership that I exercised in Asia Pacific was serving as an IP ambassador. By coordinating with the U.S. Trade Representative's Office, I pushed for IP legislation and enforcement that the U.S. and IBM desired (which were essentially identical). I invested time and energy by meeting one-on-one with officials in government, industry, and the academia to explain the U.S. IP laws with the expectation that they would emulate our laws. Such individualized meetings with the ministries in Chana and Vietnam were most notable. These officials were fascinated by how well the IP law system in the U.S. works. In particular they were eager to fully understand the U.S. copyright law and customs enforcement at our borders.

I gave formal presentations to IP organizations in

Australia, China, Hong Kong, India, Indonesia, Malaysia, Singapore, South Korea, Taiwan, and Vietnam. I wrote and published articles on various aspects of IP in Asian journals and International proceedings. Coaching and imparting knowledge on IP, internally in IBM and externally to the local communities, became a part of my leadership repertoire.

This international assignment normally was for a maximum of two years. However, I broke this practice. IBM extended my assignment for a record five years, which I attribute to my good cultural fit and job performance. I was promoted to the executive level during this assignment.

Following the international assignment, I repatriated to the IBM Microelectronics Division as the head IP Counsel where a dozen years earlier I was a newly hired and the lowest ranking attorney. As the head Counsel, I orchestrated a team of 70 employees including 30 patent attorneys to accomplish three critical annual objectives: file 1,000 patent applications; issue 1,000 patents to sustain IBM's top patent rank in the U.S.; and generate an income of $700 M–$850 M.

The last of these objectives was the most challenging which required commanding leadership and be fanatical about patent monetization. I assembled an A-team of reverse engineers, seasoned and articulate patent attorneys, know-how technicians and marketing experts who shared my fanaticism. I believed that when fanatics come together with other fanatics, the multiplicative effect is unstoppable. I distilled the complex art of patent licensing into simple components and delegated them to my team with set expectations and fostered creativity in closing deals.

Over a period of six years my team consistently met the patent filings and issuances. Importantly, my team delivered over $5 B of income which included hundreds of pure patent license deals, dozens of patent sales, and a sizable number of multiyear patent license and technology transfer deals with many domestic and foreign companies including Siemens, Infineon, Toshiba, Sony, Charter Semiconductor, Nanya, Micron, AMD and others. Technology transfer required my commanding leadership as the documentation of know-how, show-how, software and other tools and vendor lists needed to practice the patented technology were elusive and required my incessant push on the technologists who were outside my chain of command.

I was at the peak of my performance as a lawyer and supervisor. However, the stress of meeting incessant demands and the constant breathing down my neck by people from the company's Finance organization to raise more and more revenue from IP compelled me to seek a reprieve. My family also needed a change of scenery.

I asked IBM to relocate me to the more enjoyable climate of San Jose, CA which the company obliged. As the IP Research Counsel for four R&D Labs located in San Jose, Beijing, New Delhi and Tokyo, I directed the IP teams based in those locations. I was back working with the brilliant scientists in these labs marveling at the scientific breakthroughs they made in nanotechnology, new semiconductor memory devices, quantum computing, artificial intelligence and more and safeguarding the inventions they made.

Five years later, I received a call from NVIDIA Corporation in Santa Clara, CA to see whether I would be interested in patent litigation. A few years earlier NVIDIA recruited me to serve as their first IP Counsel. I was not ready to leave IBM at that time and declined NVIDIA's offer. Since I did not directly handle patent litigation at IBM, I jumped at the NVIDIA's latest overture. The litigation work was mostly defensive.

Defending patent infringement suits is never enjoyable, often emotional and a drain on company's financial resources which is the role I stepped into at NVIDIA. I quickly cultivated a leadership trait which needed courage, tenacity, aggressiveness, and perseverance. Suits filed against NVIDIA in state and federal courts and before the International Trade Commission as well as patent assertions by patent licensing entities before they commenced lawsuits required a tailored approach. With help from hired litigation counsel, I devised proven roadmaps and strategies which lead to victory or settlement.

Litigation is the sport of kings because of its expense, complexity and, for a defendant like NVIDIA, it posed interference in the freedom to operate its business. The solution that I championed of investigating the patent(s) asserted, mapping aggressive defenses against infringement, asserting solid proof of invalidity and sometimes a design around the patent's claims, minimized litigation costs and resulted in quick settlement. I received a lot of support from my colleagues in the Silicon Valley when I spoke against the patent trolls because they too suffered from such patent harassment.

After more than 4 years of vigorous litigation, I came to the conclusion that a Courtroom is not always the place to try to get ahead. There are tradeoffs between litigation and innovation and the time and resources a company spends in the Courtroom, it is not inventing. I convinced my upper management that a judicious settlement is wiser than costly and meaningless litigation with patent trolls.

Then it was time to answer the call from IGT Corporation to become their first Vice President of IP in Las Vegas and Reno, NV sites.

At IGT, I recruited and energized a strong and energetic IP team of seven attorneys and two law students in addition to IP administrators. I reinvigorated invention and patent portfolio development and monetization and put an essential end to costly and wasteful litigation that prevailed before I joined IGT.

"Innovate, team and serve" was the modus operandi that I inculcated in my staff. Two mantras of *"invent or die"* and *"patent or perish"* became my gospel among the inventor community which kick-started invention disclosure and rejuvenated patent portfolio development in my department.

I preached that invention is a spark of creativity and determined perseverance it represents.

I established written IP strategies, policies and procedures for in-house use and with external patent and trademark prosecution firms upon which IGT fully relied for protection of IP. The patent and technology monetization program that I established at IGT is the best of breed which combined the proven licensing techniques at IBM and litigation practices at NVIDIA.

Also at IGT, I helped the community by encouraging the University of Nevada Law School in Las Vegas to cultivate the habit of patent monetization by putting the university's patent portfolio to use by licensing it to businesses. With assistance from the Dean of the Law School, I championed conferences and discussions on licensing and helped fund and establish a chair titled "IGT Professor of Intellectual Property Law" which is now held by a law professor to raise awareness that UNLV is committed to Intellectual Property.

With thirty years of practice as a counselor in national and international settings, it was time to unwind. Unwinding was not quitting, as winners never quit, and quitting is hard to justify because of the sunk cost of investing my time, energy and resources into earning my five degree in multiple fields of education and a wide swath of professional experience I gained. But quitting with intentions, which is a leap forward toward my next goals, seemed acceptable.

I made a strategic decision to free up my time and energy

for things that mattered most. Like giving back to the society from which I benefited immensely and writing which I enjoy. Writing takes all of the creative juices to use and I have a limited amount of it as it competed with my need to share my skills and experiences with others in the society.

The academia, the corporate world and people from various cultures around the world shaped me to be what I am now—a persuasive, proactive and courageous counselor in advising my clients about what can go wrong and persuade them to follow the law and do the right thing from a moral, ethical and proper corporate governance perspective.

My experience extended to many roles: as a teacher, physicist, counselor, managing attorney, patent & technology license facilitator, IP litigator, patent development and portfolio manager, IP ambassador, and startup business mentor and writer. In addition, because I could articulate succinctly, I spoke extensively throughout the world on intellectual property matters.

Opportunities to give back initially arrived in the form of start-up companies which needed my ability to identify and protect the nascent IP upon which the business was founded. I made it a rule to not burden them with a salary, but some promised stock in the company for the legal services that I rendered. The services I rendered lasted for 2-3 years or more. With one startup I agreed to serve on its Board of Directors with small a payment of the company's stock.

However, none of these companies took off and my stock in them turned to be worthless. I have no regrets for servicing them as my real passion was to voluntarily contribute my knowledge and experience.

I then discovered Score which stands for Service Core of Retired Executives. Score is a national organization and is associated with the U.S. Small Business Administration. Score puts retired executives like me through a crash course passing which leads to the status of Certified Business Mentor. Score provides a forum to its Certified Business Mentors where clients from the general public who are in the throes of starting a small business can receive free advice. Score was an excellent fit for what I wanted to do—provide counselling on IP matters.

In parallel, I resumed writing which has always been my passion. My writing shifted to newspaper articles where I write on education, business, international trade, and other matters of national interest. These articles were published invariably in the Las Vegas Sun or the Las Vegas Business Press which, like the Sun, is an arm of the Las Vegas Review Journal.

An article that I wrote titled "Faculty's role in controlling tuition" which was published in Las Vegas Sun on April 19, 2014 decried the ever-increasing tuition costs for students. I challenged that our universities should be run as a business by controlling costs through efficiency of operation and suggested that faculty members monetize their intellectual property to raise revenue for the university which would ameliorate the perpetual increase in student tuition.

DECISION TO RUN FOR REGENT

What else do I do with the amalgamation of education, knowledge, and experience that I amassed? Giving it back to the community in even more ways has become my burning desire. It is with this idealistic thought that I decided to run for the position of University Regent.

Before signing up as a candidate for this position, I did research to find out what non-political positions were available in southern Nevada to run for. I was interested in an office which would enable me to freely offer my services. The regent position perfectly matched my need as it was nonpartisan and voluntary.

I came to know from the district where I reside that the incumbent regent Andrea Anderson decided not to seek reelection for her position as the regent. Ms. Anderson's decision encouraged me even more to run since I thought that I may run unopposed.

On the filing deadline of March 16, 2018, I went to the Secretary of State's office in Las Vegas, filled out the paperwork and placed myself on the official ballot as candidate for the Office of Regent, State University District 12. A day later I discovered that three other candidates were running for the same position. I looked forward to a spirited competition.

Having not run for election before, I searched for a manual which would explain the process to follow and run a successful campaign. I did not find any such and the process remained a mystery. I concluded that the incumbent Dr. Anderson would be an ideal source of information on this process. I decided to reach out to her.

Andrea Anderson was appointed by Governor Jim Gibbons to serve on the Board of Regents in 2009 and was elected by the Nevada voters in 2010 and retained in the 2012 elections as the representative from District 12. I spoke with Dr. Anderson to understand the nature of the work of a regent and what I could expect if I were to be elected to this position. She was very candid and shared useful answers to my queries, while proclaiming right up front that she is supporting another candidate (Amy Carvalho) to be her successor. While I was disappointed that I cannot ask for input on the campaign as it might pose a conflict of interest with my fellow-candidate Ms. Carvalho, I stayed with question related to the regent position. Asked as to how many hours per week will the regent position require, she candidly stated as many as you want, but 10 hours/week is typical for attending the Board meetings, four time a year, some lasting 2 days and some of which are telecast locally for participation without travel to Reno or other Nevada locations. Asked about the most challenging issue she faced as regent, it was funding: receiving funding from the state legislature, balancing the budget and getting approval of new curricula have been a challenge. She downplayed any North/South split on the Board while acknowledging that some operational issues are present. Finally I asked what benefits the regent receives in return for the unpaid service. She explained such small rewards as invitations to attend commencement exercises at Nevada colleges, passes to the Ballroom Gala of the UNLV Foundation, passes to college football games, free access to Lecture Series of the universities, attend award ceremonies, etc.

When I filed for the regent position, I was handed a stack of documents that the Secretary of State compelled me to electronically sign. These formalities included (1) a declaration for the Election department to use as well as distribute to the public of the Office for which I am a candidate, (2) A Public Information Sheet containing my name and address and date of birth, (3) an affirmation that under penalty of law and perjury that I am a qualified elector and that I have never been convicted of treason or a felony, etc., (4) Nevada Acknowledgement of Ethical Standards for Public Officers, (5) attesting to a Code of Fair Campaign Practices, albeit such subscription is indicated as voluntary, (6) agreement to electronically file on the Secretary Of State's AURORA platform my Financial Disclosure Agreement (FDA) identifying sources of income from self and household member, (7) an acknowledgement of the requirement to file electronically my Contributions & Expense Reports (C&E Reports) on five specified dates from May 22, 2018 to January 15, 2019, (8) a reminder of IRS requirement to file a form when a candidate raised $25,000 or more, etc.

Additional documents that were handed included information on how U.S. Postal Service can assist in the handling of the campaign mail, "Rules & Regulations Regarding the Placement of Political Signs" issued by the Nevada Department of Transportation as well as by the Henderson department of Building, and a request of my photograph for posting on Secretary of State's Election Night reporting website.

Promptly I submitted my FDA, my first C&E report and my photo which were immediately acknowledged. Having satisfied the initial formalities of my candidacy, I shifted my attention to a campaign platform to run upon. I wanted to shape the higher education system in the Silver State by collaborating with my fellow regents in every possible way.

My platform would simply be this: (1) Own the problems facing University regents and collectively solve them; (2) Build institution-industry partnership to develop student job skills; and (3) Cater to higher education in Science, Technology, Math, and Engineering (STEM) through a blended teaching and learning experience. I combined my platform with a succinct profile of myself which included my photograph for distribution to gain publicity of who I am, my deep educational accomplishments and intellectual capitalism which I nurtured, cultivated over decades of personal effort.

To complement my campaign, I wrote an article (Writing 19) titled "Nevada Must Educate More STEM Grads–Fast." I had it published under Expert's Corner column in the April 24, 2018 issue of the Las Vegas Business Press I wrote that STEM training is a siren call and NSHE must heed this call. I projected an immediate demand from our businesses for workers with STEM education and made a two-prong proposal: create a crash education program in our two year colleges leading to an associate degree in STEM; and establish an institution-industry collaboration to enable such program.

Writing articles gave me some public exposure, but I needed more name recognition. I explored ways to advertise my candidacy. A slew of unsolicited offers to advertise or endorse me appeared in my mail.

One such was from the Southern Nevada Central Labor Council which is affiliated with the AFL-CIO., inviting me to interview for the Regent position. The invitation included an admonition that "if you DO NOT interview with the Central Labor Council, you will not be able to receive an endorsement from the Labor Council." I spoke with Ms. Debra Berko at the Council who sent me the interview and we jointly concluded that for the regent position, I do not need an interview or endorsement.

Another solicitation was from Tim Petarra, President of Veterans in Politics Nevada Chapter. It stated that Veterans in Politics International (VIPI) will conduct Non-Judicial Endorsement Interviews and you must be present to be considered for endorsement at a specified location and time.

I tried to reach Mr. Petarra, to find out whether a non-veteran like me can expect to receive VIPI endorsement, but we could not connect.

The third solicitation was from Nevada Concerned Citizens (NCC) which is a non-profit committed to promoting the Judeo-Christian World View as a basis for family policy. A 16 item questionnaire accompanied the solicitation. From the nature of the questions, I did not see the benefit of my response to NCC.

Another solicitation was from Seniors United which is an organization concerned about issues in Nevada that may affect the senior community. The questionnaire that accompanied it was not relevant to the responsibilities of a regent and directed more to other political candidates.

Then there were numerous local and national printing companies who sent me post cards. They solicited to print yard signs, brochures, banners, invitations, car magnets, T-shirts, buttons, etc. Some quoted their rates for placing the order and offered discounts.

I contacted two of the printing companies and priced the cost of printing few dozen road signs for posting in District 12, a couple of thousand postcards printed with my photo and a brief bio on one side and the platform on which I am running for the regent on the other side as well as brochures for handing them to potential voters that I will meet. I came up with catchy slogans such as "Innovate Education–

Elect–T. Rao Coca–Regent," "For Better Education–Elect T. Rao Coca–Regent District 12", etc. The cost for printing a small number of items approached thousands of dollars.

I explored publicizing my candidacy by placing strategic advertisements in Las Vegas Review Journal. Since I need publicity only in District 12, the Journal steered me to their weekly insert of View and target its circulation to District 12–which was covered by three zones of the newspaper. Beverly Palmer at the Journal quoted that for a full page, full color ad for one zone will cost $496, which meant that it will cost me nearly $1,500/week if the View is distributed in the entire District 12. Then I entertained the thought of commissioning the Journal to print my ads on sticky notes which are affixed to the newspaper. The cost for the sticky notes for circulation in a single zone was $1,830 and proportionately increased by the number of zones.

I was surprised by the high amount of campaign money that was raised and spent by other regent candidates. An article published in the Las Vegas Sun, revealed that Dr. Mark Doubrovo, a candidate for regent from District 7, raised $100,000 to defeat his opponent Ray Rauson in 2010 who raised $16,000. Given that the regent post paid $89 a meeting for six meetings and perks such as free tickets to college football games, raising (and spending) $100,000 did not make sense. I could only conjecture that the regent post served them as a steppingstone for higher political jobs, which is not my goal.

Being pragmatic, it became clear that even a limited

advertising of my candidacy is going to be a costly proposition. I decided to have brochures printed for distribution to voters and rely on the word of mouth or other free publicity.

Since there was no established forum where candidates for the regent's office could engage in a spirited exchange of their views related to higher education, and I could receive little guidance from the Election Department or the Secretary of State's office, I decided to crash the monthly gatherings like the Boulder City Republic Women's Meeting in Boulder City which I did and made myself known to the attendees and distributed my brochure.

Likewise, I personally notified my fellow mentors at Score, my Score clients who live in District 12, fellow members of my gym, and my local friends. Restricting my campaign to voters in District 12 became somewhat complicated as many people did not know whether they lived in this District.

Then came a request form the Las Vegas Review Journal to provide my candidate information and submit written answers to specific questions related to the office that I am seeking for use in the Journal's 2018 Voter's Guide to the June 12 primary election. I furnished carefully crafted answers which were consistent with my already established campaign platform. The in-line version of the Voter's Guide featured my candidacy and became available just before the primary election.

As I was gearing up for the primary election and cast my vote during the early voting period and urged my family and friends to do the same, a lengthy article and an accompanied editorial appeared in the May 25, 2018 issue of the Las Vegas Sun. The article titled "Meet the political unknown running unopposed" was an extensive interview with Donald MeMichael, Sr. who was a candidate for regent from District 4, which serves a large part of the eastern valley of and North Las Vegas. He was running unopposed. The accompanying editorial bemoaned that *"this unknown first-time candidate–who acknowledges he wasn't expecting to win the seat when he filed and isn't sure how much of a challenge he's bitten off–is facing a clear pathway to becoming a regent."* The editorial further stated that *"for the record, being a Nevada regent is a heavy lift. Doing it right involves poring through documents hundreds of pages long on a regular basis; gaining an understanding of complexities unique to higher education, like accreditation and tenure processes; and developing a working knowledge of state and federal law applying to higher education, to name just a few of the challenges."*

The newspaper's succinct description of the duties of regent seems to perfectly match what I have done in my life and gave me more confidence that I am well prepared to serve as the regent: as a lawyer who gained admission to three state bars and the federal patent bar I have pored through thousands of pages long documents on a regular basis; as a teacher I went through the tenure and certification process; and as an educator, I successfully navigated the higher education waters domestically and internationally to secure my five university degrees in technology and law. Importantly, I have the caliber and immense interest in devoting time to serve as the regent like the newspaper editorial suggested.

However, in the primary election I was able to secure only 8% of votes compared with candidate Amy Carvalho who received the highest number (46.8%) followed by another candidate who earned 33.7%. I speculate my loss to my unknown candidacy; my inability to grease the election machine by funneling money; and voters' not taking time to review the official Voter's Guide published by the Las Vegas Review Journal and know about my candidacy before casting their vote.

While I am out of the race for the regent, I remain committed to serving the community, albeit without the prestigious title of University Regent.

22

STEALING OF U.S. INTELLECTUAL PROPERTY BY CHINA MUST STOP—ABANDON TRADE TARIFFS

Published in the Las Vegas Business Press *on August 6, 2018*

THEFT OF U.S. INTELLECTUAL property in the international arena is an act of economic war. It could be a national security issue if the stolen IP is used for military purposes against the U.S. or its allies.

Creation of intellectual property requires a huge investment of capital to build research and development centers, recruit and hire highly educated and gifted intellectuals, and establish a culture and environment where creativity is cultivated and prized. Not only does creation of IP requires a huge investment of money, but it also requires enormous patience and perseverance as many inventive ideas and creative works may not succeed on the first attempt and may require the discipline and dedication to retry until success is achieved. Many U.S. corporations in the information technology industry like IBM, Intel, and Qualcomm have excelled in IP and are regarded as role models.

After the IP is created, it is generally subjected to a virtuous cycle consisting of a assessing its technical advancement and economic value, seeking legal protection domestically and internationally (by such means as patents, copyrights, trademarks, and trade secrets), securing such legal protection, followed by exploitation of the IP for economic gain through monetization which includes litigation against thieves of the IP. The end result of this virtuous cycle is a measure of the return on investment that was made in each of the phases of the IP's virtuous cycle.

When the IP asset is created and properly secured, it may become more valuable than other assets such as the land, the R&D laboratory buildings with their attendant cumulative capital investments for equipment and the employee salaries and benefits, combined. Generally, secured IP is the last asset that remains after a business ceases to operationally exist and a bankruptcy court decides how to dispose of the IP, generally through a bankruptcy sale. For example, when Northern Telecom in Canada went into bankruptcy the sale of its portfolio of 6,000 patents fetched a cash of $6 B.

When valuable U.S. IP is stolen by rogue business groups in China, such theft is not merely an economic theft. It is a violation of the existing international agreements on trade as well as national laws which may lead to criminal penalties. Chinese entities that steal IP have completely bypassed not only the investment and resources needed for its creation, but also fully avoided significant investment in the other phases of the virtuous cycle described above. In effect, they violated the carefully crafted queue and moved to the front of the line unfairly and illegally to reap the benefits by not investing a dime, any time or human intellectual talent.

China's theft of U.S. IP is wanton, deliberate and coerced and has been going on for more than three decades and continues now despite China's present status as the second largest economy behind the U.S.

It was wanton, because when China opened up its economy to foreign investment in the late 1980's, following protests by students to democratize the country, it did not have any IP of its own to depend on. China was impatient to invest and create its own IP as pressure from its people for quick political reform mounted. The government needed to engage in Western-style industrialization in a hurry. Stealing of IP was an easy way out.

The theft was deliberate because the government engaged its state agencies and military personnel to snoop into our open business enterprises and walk away with a valuable loot of stolen IP which they used to produce products in competition with our companies.

The theft was coerced for several reasons. China forestalled legal protection for IP that U.S. companies sought from China Intellectual Property Office since it did not want the U.S. companies to have a lock on such IP. Second, the Chinese government then imposed an arbitrary rule upon foreign companies who wanted to do business in China: the foreign company must establish a 50/50 joint venture with a Chinese partner. Invariably, the Chinese partner was comprised of camouflaged military group. In fact, China controlled the workers that the JV needed. The modus operandi used for the JV to hire employees was this. A roster of personnel was offered to the foreign partner to select from. Some in this roster were spies selected by the Chinese government to steal the technology that the foreign partner possessed or transferred into the JV. In other words, the JV was a conduit for siphoning off the IP of the foreign partner.

There was one other way a U.S. entity could do business in China. This was the conventional way of exporting products made in the U.S. into China, but those products were subjected to high Chinese tariffs.

China used the JV ploy knowing full well that the U.S. companies were attracted by the cheap labor and potential size of the Chinese market and the profits they can derive from selling the products made by the JV in that market. Mesmerized by this lure of profits, many American companies ignored the fiduciary duty they owed to their stockholders and carelessly contributed the company's valuable IP to the JV without establishing proper measures to safeguard the IP from misappropriation or theft by the JV partner. These American companies also ignored their social responsibility to the U.S. by hollowing out the jobs that the American workers held and moving them to China.

Many such JV's that were formed quickly folded for one reason or another, but mainly because the Chinese partner wanted to walk away with the IP that was transferred into the JV by the U.S. partner. The Chinese partner set up an independent shop to make use of that IP solely for the benefit of the Chinese partner. This has been the root cause in China for the free technology transfer of U.S. intellectual property. Essentially, China duped the American companies to handover their IP on the pretext of establishing a JV for the mutual benefit of the U.S. and Chinese partners, but the JV was a nothing other than a sham to steal the U.S. IP.

Today, it is possible to establish a wholly foreign owned enterprise to do business in China. The WFOE has a better control over its IP, but stealing of the IP continues in other ways, for example, by unscrupulous Chinese hires. However, the 50/50 JV is still encouraged by the Chinese Communist Party particularly when it comes to U.S. banks and financial firms.

The U.S. Trade Representative which just completed a seven-month investigation into China's intellectual property theft found that the Chinese theft of American IP currently costs between $225 B and $600 B annually. Extrapolating this metric to the last thirty years of theft, the costs run to $675 billion to 1.8 trillion. This ill-gotten wealth from America propelled China into the #2 economy. The theft of IP by China is not limited to the U.S. China systematically stole IP from many other western countries who possessed valuable technology as they followed U.S. footsteps into China.

As a result of this technology theft, gleaming skyscrapers and modern infrastructure was built in many cities across China and it became industrialized in a short span of two decades.

Several imitators of U.S. companies are now flourishing in China. To name a few, Huawei is an imitator of Cisco; Baidu is an imitator of Google, Xiomi is an imitator of Apple, Alibaba is a copycat of Amazon, etc. These imitators are in the business of offering products in competition with products exported to China by the U. S. companies. In fact, since the Chinese companies stole the technology and did not invest any capital for its creation or development, they are able to undercut the U.S. companies and many times shut them out of business in China all together.

Adding insult, the Chinese government continues to apply high tariffs on goods exported from the U.S. in order to protect their domestic industry, which also happens to be heavily subsidized by the government.

The tariffs imposed by China are in violation of the trade agreements under treaties such as the World Trade Organization. China pays scant respect for such agreements, particularly when it comes to fairness and reciprocity which are key ingredients of international trade.

The court system in China is biased in favor of its citizens and companies. When U.S. plaintiffs go to court in China for violation of their IP, winning is difficult. Even when they win the suits the monetary damages awarded by the Chinese courts have been miniscule compared to those awarded by the U.S. courts for theft of similar IP.

How does U.S. solve a problem like China?

China is now an economic power. It should behave in commensurate with its stature by reforming its behavior to conform to international standards. Reciprocity and fairness should take the center stage in everything that China does that economically affects other countries. Here are some additional and specific suggestions:

1. End the theft of IP from U.S. firms who do business in China and end it on the American soil.

2. Stop enticing U.S. companies to establish 50/50 joint ventures with Chinese partners. Instead, encourage the American company to have 100% ownership of its business in China. Allow such WFOE to recruit its employees without the heavy handed government intervention.

3. Grant full legal protection of IP of U.S. firms in China by ending local judicial protectionism and bias against the U.S. firms.

4. Reform the Chinese Intellectual Property Courts to apply existing laws without bias against foreigners. Enhance criminal punishment and award of monetary damages for infringement of IP.

5. Respect and abide by the decisions over disputes, whether on trade or territorial issues, with foreign

countries by dispute resolution centers like the The Hague tribunal, the United Nations International Court of Justice and the WTO.

6.   Reform trade barriers like the imposition of tariffs to render them mutually equal and reciprocal.

7.   Level the playing field by ending government subsidies to industries which export products.

8.   When the U.S. government reduces or drops trade tariffs all together, reciprocate like behavior.

If China follows these measures it will go a long way to lessen the trade tensions with the U.S. When it comes to trade, fairness and reciprocity must be practiced by China. This is what the U.S. expects.

23

IT'S TIME FOR COMPANIES TO BRING JOBS HOME

Published as a Guest Column in the Las Vegas Sun *on Nov. 24, 2018*

THE ENACTMENT OF the 2017 Tax Cuts and Jobs Act that went into effect on Jan. 1, 2018 is bound to kindle a renaissance of the U.S. manufacturing base.

Under the act, the corporate tax rate has been lowered to 21 percent from 35 percent. One-time repatriation of profits earned by multinational U.S. companies by their overseas subsidiaries is taxed at 13.5 percent for cash and 8 percent on other assets.

U.S. multinational corporations had accumulated nearly $2.6 trillion offshore as of the end of 2017, much of it in tax-haven countries. The act encourages companies to bring money back to the U.S. at these lower rates.

Many U.S. companies have already committed to significant repatriation amounts. Apple has $252 billion in cash alone on its balance sheet stashed overseas, and it pledged to pay $38 billion in tax on repatriated income over the next eight years. Other big businesses like Microsoft, Alphabet, Cisco and Oracle have a significant chunk of their profit in cash parked overseas.

The Bureau of Economic Analysis reported that over $305 billion has returned to the U.S. from overseas accounts. The repatriated stash is now available in the U.S. for companies to invest, pay out dividends, bonuses, and stock buybacks, establish new development and manufacturing centers, and hire new workers.

With growth of 4.2 percent in the third fiscal quarter and 3.5 percent this quarter, our economy is firing on all cylinders.

In other words, a renaissance of manufacturing is in the offing. The recent announcement to levy trade tariffs on goods imported into the U.S. is also motivating U.S. and foreign companies to establish their manufacturing plants in the U.S. to avoid payment of such tariffs. The Taiwanese Foxconn Technology Groups decision to invest $10 billion to establish a manufacturing campus in Wisconsin to create 13,000 jobs is an example to revitalize the semiconductor manufacturing base on our shores.

Likewise, foreign automobile companies are investing more money into their previously established U.S. plants to expand capacity or to start new plants.

Labor costs in foreign countries are rising, which is another reason why U.S. manufacturers are returning jobs to the United States. Yet another reason is that regulation has been dramatically reduced. All of these factors have contributed to rising optimism among American manufacturers.

It is time for U.S. corporations to demonstrate not just their fiduciary duty but also social, ethical, moral and patriotic duties and bring back the jobs they are harboring overseas.

It is incumbent upon them to establish hardware and software development and manufacturing campuses in our country and, where needed, retrain the U.S. workforce for the jobs that the economy calls for as part of the quid pro quo for the lower corporate tax rate, the tax holiday on the repatriated profits, and deregulation. With the U.S. jobless rate at 3.7 percent in September, businesses have no choice but to spend to upgrade existing and new employee skills to meet their specific needs. Such investment would promote loyalty.

U.S. companies should revitalize not only the high technology industries, but also the basic industries that have been outsourced to other countries. For example, nuts, bolts and fasteners are critical components upon which higher-level products such as aircraft, space vehicles, automobiles, railroads, computers, smartphones and household appliances depend upon. The nuts and bolts are the weakest link in the chain and must be produced within our country to ensure their quality, integrity, dependability, and ready availability. We have for too long depended on such nuts and bolts components coming from China, India, Taiwan and other countries. With 3D printing using nanoparticles in rapid development for critical components, it is imperative that we regain our footing in this manufacturing.

Likewise, automobile products are critical to our economy, particularly as the production of the automobiles continues to increase. The ready availability of such parts is critical for repairing used cars.

U.S. oil companies should enhance their capital expenditure and improve efficiency of operations with high technology in fracking to generate more oil and wean out our dependence on OPEC.

In other words, the expected renaissance should address every aspect of our manufacturing needs and avoid dependence on any foreign country, no matter how friendly they are now. Self-reliance is the key for U.S. manufacturing. We should restore our manufacturing economy to the 1965 level, when it accounted for 53 percent of the economy.

All U.S. companies, as well as foreign companies that wish to do business in this country and profit from it, should participate in this renaissance and revitalize the U.S. manufacturing base. Revitalization of our GDP beyond the current levels should be their goal.

24

COVID-19: CHINA'S INADVERTENT WMD AGAINST HUMANITY

Published as a post in LinkedIn on April 1, 2020

THE WORLD KNOWS now that the central Chinese city of Wuhan and capital of Hubei is the epicenter and place of origin of coronavirus which infected nearly a million people globally (as of this writing).

The Chinese authorities launched a concerted campaign to question the origin of this virus. At first, they attempted to blame 17 athletes from the U.S. Armed Forces who participated in the Military World Games held during October 18 to 27, 2019 in Wuhan. However, they offered no evidence to support it. Another theory they advanced, without again any evidence, is to divert its origin to Africa.

There were rumors that the virus was made in a laboratory or otherwise engineered in China. However, according to the findings published in the journal of *Nature Medicine*, the virus is a product of natural evolution possibly from an animal source.

China reported the coronavirus to the World Health Organization on December 26, 2019, yet it may have been circulating in Wuhan as early as November 17. China's recalcitrance to timely acknowledge coronavirus and failure to take necessary steps to contain its own population in Wuhan cost the world community two precious months to respond.

The Chinese authorities not only lied about the date of inception of the virus but failed to report the true statistics of the number of people in China that were infected. They did not report how many of these infected people travelled to foreign countries like South Korea, northern Italy, Iran, USA and others and infected those foreigners until well after the discovery of the infection and deaths by the foreign countries. When China reported such statistics, they obfuscated and had every reason to cover up the true numbers. The Chinese treated their statistics as gold when in fact it was a made-up trash, lending credence to the belief that one should never trust data from dictators.

China did not behave like a civilized and ethical country. Certainly, it fell short of behaving like the second highest economic powerhouse in the world. It failed to show leadership during this crisis but inflamed it by failing to respond in a timely and open manner that occurred in its own backyard. It showed scant regard to the rest of the world in spreading the most dangerous epidemic. In fact, China by its failure to act unleashed a weapon of mass destruction. There is no end in sight for the number of deaths around the world because of this epidemic.

It is a disgrace that China failed to learn from America's

demonstrated leadership during times of crises around the world far from its shores. An economic power like China that failed to be inspired by America's past leadership tells volumes about the character of China.

Besides this colossal human suffering and death, the *Wall Street Journal* reported that China is now hurriedly collecting more than $200 billion from overseas lending. China loaned this money, as opposed to giving it as foreign aid, to many emerging markets to have infrastructure and other projects completed for them. These borrowers are now at the risk of drowning in debt while coping for their survival in the coronavirus epidemic.

Pakistan, a steadfast ally of China because of Beijing's One Belt One Road project now underway which stretches through the Pakistani territory is a complete captive of China. Pakistan now teeters on the edge of potential human disaster with the coronavirus not only because of its debt obligations to China, but also because its Prime Minister Imran Khan refused to quarantine infected Pakistani's or impose social distance.

India reportedly is indebted to China in excess of $50 billion for various unsound commercial and infrastructure projects now underway in India. China's motivation for this massive funding is to secure access to the Indian markets. With a population of over 1.3 billion, India is under a harsh lock down termed as the people's curfew because of China's coronavirus epidemic. India is ensnared in a debt trap that leaves it vulnerable to China's influence. If China were to continue its pattern of arm twisting to collect the borrowed money from India, it could lead to a major hit for its economy and may eventually lead to a military confrontation.

Many of the overseas projects that China is engaged in are supposedly by the private sector. However, the separation between private enterprise and state-owned enterprise in China is blurry. When it comes to collection of debt owed to a private enterprise, the Chinese government subtly steps in to exercise its muscle.

America is too dependent on China for many essential goods, particularly medicine and basic medical supplies like face masks, gloves, gowns, and ventilators, as this epidemic has demonstrated. One important lesson for America to learn from this epidemic is to move the supply chain for medicine back to our shores. By outsourcing to China, America has become too dependent on many other essential goods as well including parts for airplanes, ships, railroads and automobiles which keep our transportation industry humming. While the American consumer enjoyed low prices for such goods made in China because of the lower labor cost over there, the American labor force suffered a huge loss of their jobs over the last three decades. Unwittingly, we transferred our technology secrets and know-how to China to have those products manufactured or alternatively China outright stole such intellectual property from us through espionage. While bringing such jobs back to America and weaning away from our dependence on supply chains from China may seem like protectionism, it now is now a matter of our survival and national security

Without America's vast purchases of goods from China, the Chinese economy will suffer. A similar movement is afoot in Europe. If these movements by the West as a whole were to take hold then the Chinese economy will stagnate and in due course will collapse. That will be a good outcome for America because we can spend less on our military industrial complex and rebuild our country's physical and manufacturing infrastructure to become self-dependent and self-sufficient worrying less about our national security.

25

IS AMERICA STUPID? MY CONVERSATIONS WITH AUSTRALIANS

Published as a post in LinkedIn on April 21, 2020

I AND MY WIFE are avid travelers. Travel has been my avocation ever since my childhood years. We travelled around the world several times. In the past we travelled by getting on airplanes and making our own arrangements for stays in hotels and sight-seeing. Learning about the history, culture and food of the country we visited was our passion. It satisfied us more than anything else. Lately we have been cruising, as booking with a cruise line takes away the burden of making hotel reservations and other arrangements on the ground to see places. Cruising has its own charm although now with the coronavirus pandemic that is razing it is being shunned.

While on the cruise ship I always look to engage with fellow cruisers to have a productive dialog and understand their lives and the region and country from which they hailed. We ask for the Anytime Dining routine which means we can go at any time of the evening and sit with different people each time at the dining table. By dining with different people each evening gives us an opportunity to meet more people and understand points of view of our fellow-diners. The topics that come up for discussion are somewhat limitless.

Being curious, I sometimes bring up topics that are stimulating to me. While I seldom bring up religion and politics as they are taboo for discussion with strangers, I probe them on such topics as the educational system, the tax burden on citizens, immigration, the health care practice, the legal system and, in general, the state of affairs in their country.

We just completed a 46-day cruise on the Sun Princess from Fremantle, Australia to Cape Town, South Africa and back. This ship with more than 2,200 passengers was dominated by Australians. Less than 100 passengers were American which was unusual as most of the other cruise ships that we travelled on were dominated by Americans. The majority of the Australians were old, many in wheelchairs and walkers. Almost all seemed to be at the high end of obesity and they seldom missed four meals a day including the afternoon tea with fattening cookies and cakes. The Australians are prone to imbibe a lot, much more than passengers from other countries. The bars on the ship were generally occupied by them more than by any other nationality group. The Aussies tend to be boisterous especially after a few shots of vodka or scotch or a pack of beer.

On the fifth day as we were sailing in the India Ocean on the way to Cape Town via Singapore, we sat with three other couples for dinner in a well laid out table with a clean white table cloth, linen and fine cutlery. We introduced ourselves at the table to the other guests. Some of us at the table were proud to talk about their present or past careers. Sure enough I talked about my profession as a corporate Intellectual Property Attorney. Just then, the Australian gentleman who was seated with his charming wife across the table from me piped up to proclaim that he worked at CSIRO in Canberra. Obviously, he wanted to draw my attention to him. A pleasant discussion followed by my asking whether he was employed with CSIRO in the early 1990's. He replied "no." I said that I had dealings with CSIRO in the nineties in my professional capacity.

I was familiar with CSIRO. It stands for Commonwealth Scientific and Industrial Research. It is an Australian federal agency responsible for scientific research. While claiming that CSIRO is a non-profit organization, this government agency is interested in making money and sometimes plays hardball over pricing and is known to fight in courts to enforce its intellectual property rights. In the early 1990's I clashed with CSIRO in Sydney.

CSIRO is now supposedly working on data privacy and artificial intelligence and machine learning, but historically they were not known to play by the book. In the early nineties CSIRO attempted to skirt the existing multilateral treaties of the Universal Copyright Convention and the Berne Convention on Copyrights even though Australia was a signatory to these treaties. What is the reason? CSIRO was behind the curve in software development compared

to some well-known American companies. CSIRO attempted to push for de-compilation of software in violation of
these treaties. This was the context in which I clashed with
CSIRO in the 1990's on behalf of IBM as I was then IBM's
Chief Intellectual Property Counsel for Asia Pacific region
which included Australia. CSIRO wanted to reverse compile
the software and essentially copy such software which was
developed after investing millions of dollars by the American companies including IBM and leapfrog over them in
their business. However, CSIRO's attempt to legalize reverse
compilation of software failed.

I was also aware that in 1996 CSIRO procured an overly
broad wireless LAN (local area network) patent in the U.S.
(# 5,487,069) and hit up many American companies. A part
of the LAN patent was allegedly incorporated in IEEE 802.11
standard. CSIRO failed to participate in the setting of the
802.11 standard, but it claimed that it "invented the Wi-Fi."
This Australian agency collected over $400 million through
settlements with the defendant American companies after
filing patent infringement suits in Federal District Court in
the Eastern District of Texas. Some people see CSIRO as one
of the "good guys" in patent suits, but others classify them
as a patent troll that stifles technology advancement. CSIRO
has been funding its existence at the expense of everyone
else who used similar wireless technology. The '069 patent
expired in 2013.

I did not bring up any of CSIRO's parlay of its WLAN

patent into income at the dinner table. I wanted the discussion to be congenial and pleasant. However, the Australian gentlemen sitting across the table from me, let me call him Robin (as he looked like the 17ᵗʰ century heroic outlaw Robin Hood who stole from the rich to pay the poor), continued to pierce his laser-sharp looks at me throughout the dinner.

The next day, as we routinely do before diner, my wife and I were sitting in a low sofa and having martinis in the Crooners bar at the mid-deck of the ship near the piazza. Crooners bar has always been our favorite place to listen to live music and imbibe wonderful James Bond martinis. As we were enjoying our martini Robin, who was apparently sitting close by and who we did not notice, darted to me with an unexpected and uncalled-for accusation of "Americans are stupid!" He did not at first qualify his statement, but just blurted out which was audible to many others in the bar who were enjoying their drinks, including Bob and Eileen from San Diego, CA who we met earlier on the ship and who also frequented the Crooners bar for martinis like we did.

Robin's provocation surprised me. Standing near me, Robin then started to mouth off that Americans are illiterate and that we don't know how to invent. That is when I decided to stand up and end his tirade by talking down at me. Robin was short. Although I was slightly less than six feet with my shoes on, I felt that I dwarfed him in height after I stood up. I told him that Australians are known to focus on esoteric and worthless technologies which never see the day of light. I told him that I base this statement on my personal experience at IBM.

IBM had an ongoing program called External Submissions under which outsiders can submit their inventions on a non-confidential basis for consideration of implementation by the company in its products. I reviewed many inventions that were submitted by Australian inventors to this program. Almost all of them seemed to be "pie-in-the-sky" types and have been conceived by people who were inebriated. During my time in the Asia Pacific Assignment none of those submitted inventions by the Australian were accepted by IBM. They were discarded as junk!

I also reminded Robin how CSRIO in the early 1990's was attempting to skirt the world treaties on Intellectual Property to steal American software technology by engaging in software de-compilation. I told him that this was an example of Australia's tacit admission that they were not innovative then, which perhaps may have changed now for the better.

After my stand against him, Robin quickly ducked and slid back into the chair where he was sitting.

Immediately, Bob came to me and remarked "I saw this guy dart to you. I heard your conversation. If I were you, I would have given him the middle finger" and made a gesture using the middle finger of his right hand. "You were being gentlemen. I am proud of you" Bob added.

Robin's point-blank accusation that American's are stupid made me think about our country and our people.

I pondered whether there is truth in what he said. After returning home from this long cruise I conducted research to seek an answer to his allegation.

When it comes to innovation and entrepreneurship, particularly in science and technology, America tops every nation in the world. We have the benefit of many brilliant scientists from Europe who migrated for various reasons to the U. S. during the periods between the two World Wars. They contributed to our leadership in science and technology particularly in building the first atomic bomb which ended the horrible Second World War.

After the Soviet Union set off the sputnik's launch in 1957, America jumped in with both feet in the space race. That brought more innovation propelling us to be the un-mistakable leader. This innovation has been the key to our prosperity and advanced our economy to be the number one in the world.

We are not illiterate as Robin asserted. Our literacy rate is in the upper nineties. Of late there is a feeling among some Americans that we are slipping behind in math and science education in our schools and colleges which in the past propelled us to the top. However, in the past such dearth of talent in math and science in our own population was compensated by immigrants from other countries particu-larly from India, Korea and Taiwan who eventually become naturalized citizens and added to our gene pool.

An analysis of the patents granted, which is a good

barometer of a nation's innovation, shows that America's long-term dominance in the number of patents granted has come to an end recently. For the first time the U.S. inventors earned less patents than the non-U. S. inventors.

Another data point is that now only a third of American employees have a science or technology job which also is the lowest in a while.

Yet our entrepreneurship never seems to slow down. The Silicon Valley, where entrepreneurism is prized, continues to thrive with private capital continuing to pour billions of dollars to make our innovation come to fruition. Thanks to the many skilled and highly educated U.S.-born graduates and immigrants that America continues to encourage immigrating to our country we continue enjoy the contribution made to our economy by this talented pool.

While America is technologically superior and we boast how smart we are as a nation, our collective belief sometimes demonstrates the opposite. Many books have been written illuminating how stupid we are. Some books like "Unusually Stupid America" written by Kathryn Petras and Ross Petras is hilarious. Many articles have been written self-deprecating and poking fun at ourselves for stupidity.

We tend to cling to beliefs that are untrue. Examples abound. Many of us continue to believe that Nazi Holocaust never happened. Many of us do not know that we have three branches in our federal government; and those who know cannot name all three branches. We lack the understanding of

Newton's law of gravity and continue to believe that the Sun orbits the earth. We deny climate change. Some Americans think that the position a couple chooses during love making can dictate the gender of the baby. When it comes to world's geography a vast majority cannot identify Iran, Iraq or Israel on a map. Even to handle simple math in their jobs, some of our workers seem to petrify. We have a minority group in America which does not believe in medicine and relies on prayer for cure of deceases they contract even in these days when the COVID-19 pandemic is raging.

When it comes to politics, the majority of us believe the television news channel they watch is telling the truth without probing its veracity and truthfulness. In this regard we are gullible to believe the media and deeply stupid and Robin is probably right, although he did not qualify that American are stupid when it comes to politics alone.

Returning to my cruise on the Sun Princess, during the course of the next forty days, I met a number of other Australians many of them in the Horizon Court where the buffet style meals are served. I engaged in one-on-one conversations with them and dwelled into a number of interesting topics for discussion. In these conversations, at times I ventured into politics with them either because they voluntarily brought up the topic or I broached politics after I sensed their political leaning.

Almost everyone knew about our President. Many liked him and some did not. I did not discuss politics with the latter, except ask for the information source upon which they relied to dislike our President. Many said it was CNN, at which point I did not discuss politics with them any further.

All had a superficial understanding of what was now going on in the U.S. from the various sources of news that was being beamed on the cruise ship's TV. Understandably, while they could mention by name the top presidential candidates who were running in the ongoing primaries of the Democratic Party, they did not know the real shakers and movers of this party. They simply referred to them as the opposition party. They could not understand what the fuss was all about with the ongoing trial to impeach our President.

I explained in some detail how our federal government was set up to function and the unfounded allegations that were launched by the opposition party, which controlled our lower House of Representatives, against a duly elected President. I explained the nitty-gritty of the American politics that led to the impeachment hearings. I explained how the opposition party hung on to a minor remark by our President in an official phone call with the President of Ukraine before he authorized sending to Ukraine a huge amount of American military aid; and the opposition party twisted this phone conversation beyond recognition and held a sham kangaroo court hearing in our lower House and drew up stupid articles of impeachment. These articles were rightfully rejected by our upper House, controlled by the President's party, thereby ending the impeachment.

After my explanation and reasoning, the Australians' consistent and uniform conclusion was that the Americans are wasting their time. Some said that Americans are being stupid. I whole-heartedly agreed with them but offered them this correction: *"Some* Americans are stupid!"

The Australians laughed. One responded, "So are we."

26

THE UNITED STATES OF NORTH AMERICA

Published as a post on LinkedIn on May 28, 2020

THE RECENTLY EXECUTED trade agreement between the major North American neighbors, the United States, Mexico and Canada, now known as the USMCA, enhances cooperation on trade, security, immigration, and public health between these neighbors. The United States is now at a crossroad having been burnt by its dangerous dependence on China for basic supply chains for protective equipment and medicines during the COVID-19 epidemic. The supply chains from China are proving to be a huge risk for the U.S. health, safety and security.

The trade war that the U.S. is now engaged with China is likely to turn ugly which will compound the threats our country is facing. Globalization that the U.S. promoted over three decades ago has proven to be a failure and it is no longer necessary. Many U.S. corporations are now thinking about rebuilding our manufacturing base on our soil and wean away from dependence on unreliable sources like China.

It is now an appropriate time to build the USMCA into a more integrated and seamless network to further reinforce the cooperation set forth in the USMCA. The time is now ripe to integrate the United States, Mexico and Canada into a single democratic country–the United Sates of North America. The USNA with a combined population of just below five hundred million will become a self-dependent economic powerhouse with territorial security, unparalleled peace and prosperity for the well-being of its new population unmatched to any other country on earth.

One of the main problems that the U.S. has been fighting against for the last half a century is the illegal immigration from our southern neighbor. The American people are divided on the immigration issue. The left-leaning citizens wants an open border and unlimited amnesty, whereas the right wants a sealed border with a wall erected between the two countries and limited amnesty. By eliminating the border with Mexico, under the concept of USNA, the division between the right and left will be solved. People would move freely, and the immigration problem would be solved instantaneously. The drug and human trafficking and other crimes associated with illegal immigration will also end.

Many synergies exist in this integration plan. Many U.S. companies now conduct business in all three countries. Many U. S. companies have manufacturing facilities in Mexico and in Canada due to lower labor costs and other reasons such as the geographic proximity which is more desirable for purposes of trade than an Asia-based manufacturer. Besides manufacturing, there exists among the neighbors a lot of commonality driven by the U.S. in healthcare, banking, telecom, broadcasting, airlines, energy, and agriculture. By eliminating the borders, these industries will thrive in a synergistic fashion and make USNA a powerful country in the world.

In terms of natural resources, USNA will be bountiful with the natural mineral resources of Canada, oil reserves of Mexico, the Athabasca tar sands of Canada and the U.S. with its vast reserves of underground oil in Alaska and the shale oil which is booming now through fracking and producing more than a million barrels of oil per day. The integrated country will be energy independent and may become a net exporter of energy and likely weaken the present oil hegemony by Saudi Arabia and Russia.

A lot of work needs to be done to make the political integration of these three proud countries possible. The first step is to have a memorandum of understanding between the leaders of the U.S., Mexico and Canada for such integration. Next, call for a Constitutional Convention in which legal scholars from the three countries participate to lay out a vision for the USNA by taking the best practices from each of the countries. Draw up a framework that reflects the best and workable aspects that have been enshrined in the respective Constitutions and which have been tested. In this vein life, liberty, pursuit of happiness and freedom of speech limited against subversion of the nation should be the pillars of the new democratic state.

By eliminating the borders with Mexico and Canada,

goods, services, and people would move more freely. The formation of a new perimeter of USNA extending in the Far North that lies to the north of the Arctic Circle combined now with Alaska and in the south to Latin America and separated by the Atlantic and Pacific Oceans on the side will bring about a geographically secure nation. The combination of natural and human resources will bring about economic expansion far beyond each of the triumvirate countries is now enjoying.

The diverse races and cultures of the people of U.S., Mexico and Canada is bound to enhance their collective creativity and innovation by leaps and bounds. Particularly if a common language spoken by the majority (namely, English) is selected as the official language and entrepreneurism and capitalism are made the cornerstones of the new country, USNA will emerge as an envy of the world. Certainly, the United States of North America will be the greatest nation on earth!

27

WORKING FROM HOME IS AN ENDURING SHIFT THAT BUSINESSES SHOULD EMBRACE

Published in Las Vegas Sun *on June 6, 2020*

THE DAYS OF office-centric employment seem to be on the wane as COVID-19 dramatically and permanently changes the way we work. Instead, work from home is going to be the new normal. The transition to work from home has been made possible by newly available technologies such as Zoom's Video Communications, Facebook's Workplace and Microsoft's Teams software. These software products offer the capabilities of high bandwidth, high-speed communication and secure encryption, which make it easy to work from anywhere in the world and seamlessly, connect with co-workers and managers under the concept of distributed work.

Corporate executives Mark Zuckerberg of Facebook and Jack Dorsey of Twitter and Square announced that tens of thousands of their company jobs will go to remote work over the next five to 10 years. The CEOs have seen merit in working from home, as it solves many problems they and their employees face, particularly by having their offices located in high-rent areas like the Silicon Valley and New York City.

Google is encouraging its employees to continue to work from home until the end of the year. Its CEO, Sundar Pichai, offered employees $1,000 each to purchase equipment and office furniture to work from home.

There are many advantages to working from home for employers. The company does not need lofty office space and furniture for workers. No longer do they need to provide tons of tangible on-premises cafeteria/kitchen food and bar services, laundry services, gym facilities and the like for employees, which have become an expected norm to Silicon Valley companies to retain talent. No need to provide expensive parking facilities. With the elimination or reduction of such souped-up workspaces and services, the employer will reap enormous savings in business expenses.

The old way of commuting to and from the office by utilizing hours that could be otherwise productively spent on work will be a plus for both the employee and the employer.

There is no need for the employees and their families to live in the prohibitively expensive homes in the Silicon Valley or New York City, but can instead move to lower-cost cities. The employee can live in lower-tax states within the U.S. or in another country and carry out the assigned work remotely. This is a tremendous advantage for the employee.

Still, the gift of working from home may be a wolf in sheep's clothing. Zuckerberg clarified that those employees who flee to lower-cost areas may have their compensation adjusted based on their home location, for example.

Another disadvantage of working from home is that it removes in-person collaboration and connection. It will be difficult to manage and mentor employees who work from home. It may also bring about potential burn-out and mental health issues if employees are isolated for an extended period. And those are just a few of the drawbacks.

But as more and more businesses move to the digital economy and online operations, working from home will become more accepted and embraced by the employer, employee and online customer. Such a business model has been proven during the COVID-19 shutdown to be highly profitable to Amazon, Shopify, Walmart, Target and a host of other companies.

The remote work strategy will offer employers the opportunity to access the best talent worldwide for the lowest salary they can pay. A ramification of working from home is that high-tech companies do not need to depend on sponsoring or accepting highly skilled H1-B visa workers from overseas. Such foreign-based workers can work from their home country for a substantially lower salary to perform the same job if a deal can be structured properly without violating the U.S. Export Control laws. This works perfectly with our government's embargo imposed on granting visas to foreigners and restrictions on travel into the United States.

With improvements in workplace software, the work-from-home digital economy will be the new normal. More companies big and small will move online and avoid the static concept of the office-centric workplace. It is time for businesses to get used to this shift and be prepared to reap the benefits of the new economy based on the reality of employees working remotely from home.

28

AMERICA BENEFITS BY BRINGING BUSINESSES HOME

Published in the Las Vegas Sun *on July 18, 2020*

GLOBAL SUPPLY CHAIN disruptions brought on by COVID-19 are prompting American companies that offshored U.S. manufacturing to consider bringing it back home—a trend known as reshoring.

We hear concern about doing business in China among members of Congress who have not been vocal in the past about the need to have dependable supply chains. China's lack of transparency and accountability in the aftermath of COVID-19 woke us up. American companies are being urged to bring manufacturing closer to home.

Offshoring (in the name of globalization) has taken place for nearly half a century and was caused by companies being seduced by the lower cost of labor in foreign countries, especially those in Asia. Offshoring started with Japan and spread to Taiwan, South Korea, Singapore and Malaysia before settling in China.

Globalization made American companies more profitable, provided our consumers with affordable products and propelled our economy. The greed to maximize profits drove the exportation of many U.S. jobs and essentially resulted in deindustrialization of the U.S. It was highly lucrative to American companies that amassed huge profits from overseas production and sales. They sheltered those profits abroad.

America generally received the better end of the bargain in globalization with Asian countries. However, lately it seems to have become a victim when it came to China.

America awakened a sleeping giant when President Richard Nixon visited China in 1972 with a policy to liberalize its economy. Subsequently, every president embraced China with the hope of integrating it as a member of the world community. All of them believed that a free market-oriented China would become internationally reasonable, or perhaps even democratic.

Instead, China played the globalization game on its own terms and with self-interest. While entering into treaties like the World Trade Organization, China violated them by forcing technology transfer as quid pro quo for doing business on its soil. What became the norm were unfair trade practices such as asymmetrical deals which benefited the domestic businesses, providing state subsidies to manufacture goods and dumping such subsidized goods on the U. S. market, and restricting importation of American goods into China.

At first, China's noncompliance was ignored by our government, which only encouraged such transgressions. No

American president confronted the Chinese Communist Party, which is known to control every move in China with the ideology of totalitarianism.

The U.S. may not be able to change China's behavior through persuasion or threats. Instead, our strategy should be to reboot our economy on our soil and lead it to recovery. The recent U.S.-China trade dispute and the COVID-19 pandemic are accelerating our companies to reshore and duplicate supply chains closer to home.

There is another motivation that is accelerating reshoring. The 2017 U.S. Tax Cut and Jobs Act enabled a portion of over $3 trillion of profits held overseas by American companies to return home tax-free. Because of the drop in economic activity caused by COVID-19, the repatriation of foreign profits surged to $124 billion in the first quarter of 2020, according to the U.S. Department of Commerce. The purpose behind the act was to encourage companies to use the repatriated profits to create jobs at home.

With the current pro-business drive by Washington galvanized by the elimination of many government regulations that plagued businesses in the past, it is increasingly attractive now to reindustrialize America.

In the wake of COVID-19, new legislation is pending in the Senate, such as the Forging Operational Resistance to Chinese Expansion Act, which among others would provide tax breaks to pharmaceutical and medical supply companies moving their operations from China to the U.S.

While the many incentives that our government is offering are laudable, it is important that our companies should help to get our house in order so we become self-dependent and self-sufficient. Our companies should show their social responsibility to our country.

U.S. companies realize the benefits of bringing manufacturing back home. The reindustrialized company would have better control over their intellectual property and manufacturing know-how, as this property would remain in-house. The company would have a dependable supply chain for products since they would be produced here. Importantly, skilled jobs result from domestic production. American workers are among the most productive in the world. With investment in smart technology and cutting-edge tools and workforce development of their skills, productivity would be high. This would usher in the 21st-century modernization of American industry.

These benefits would be somewhat offset by higher wages and meeting stricter labor, occupational safety and environmental standards, which may eat into profits. The consumer may have to pay more for products made in the USA, which many people may not mind.

Also, the newly signed U.S. trade agreement with Mexico and Canada (USMCA) is an opportune time for American companies to partner closely with companies located across our borders to reshore manufacturing and establish supply chains in North America. Mexico and Canada may be able to fill the vacuum created by curtailing our dependence on China. The USMCA improves the investment opportunity and creates more certainty of our supply chains.

29

CRISIS DRIVES AMERICA

Published as a post in LinkedIn on July 20, 2020

AMERICA SEEMS TO require a crisis to galvanize our nation into action. As a nation we do not seem to foresee impending problems and take preparatory steps to avoid or mitigate them. This is true even with our mighty military on which we spend more than one-sixth of our annual federal budget and expect to protect our nation. Examples abound when a crisis befell on us which compelled us to react.

Before the Second World War the sneak aerial attack in 1941 by the Japanese on the U.S. military base at Pearl Harbor spurred us to react. Our military intelligence did not anticipate this attack. That attack precipitated us to jump and succeed in a race to build the first atomic bomb, drop it on Hiroshima and Nagasaki and end the War.

The 9/11 attack in 2001 of the World Trade Center and the Pentagon by utilizing our civilian airplanes which were commandeered by al Queda terrorists, motivated us to invade Afghanistan to capture its mastermind and financier Osama bin Laden. Our military eventually killed him in Pakistan. Unfortunately in this quest, we sidestepped our mission and invaded Iraq on the belief that its leader Saddam Hussain was developing a weapon of mass destruction. We are still mired in those costly wars.

This year's coronavirus epidemic which originated in Wuhan, China and spread across the world including the U.S. is a crisis-provoking upheaval. The Microsoft founder Bill Gates five years ago warned us of the potential for such a worldwide epidemic, but our nation did not pay heed and was unprepared.

The immediate aftermath of the coronavirus was the cut-off by China of the supply chains for personal protective equipment and medicines to America. This act was a rude awakening to us. This silent epidemic as of this writing killed nearly 150,000 and infected close to four million Americans.

As we face more deaths and infection caused by this virus and destruction of our economy, the strategy we adopt and actions we take to overcome this crisis and avoid its repetition are crucial.

In the politically polarized state America is in, luckily when it comes to China, both political parties seem to be on the same page. They both acknowledge the origin and spread of the coronavirus is from China and the role China played to hurt American people and economy. There is agreement between our party leaders that America can no longer rely on China for our critical supply chains and a rearrangement is needed. In fact, a Cold War with China has started.

We are now entering a new era akin to what happened under President Roosevelt who after the Depression of the

1930's embraced creation of jobs under his New Deal which led to the first wave of major industrialization of America. After the Second World War from 1944-1960 we were enormously confident and prospered by harnessing capitalism for the benefit of our people. Because of the Great Society of the 1960's we instituted public healthcare entitlements of Medicare and Medicaid and have been paying a price. The baby boomers eroded the confidence we had in America because of the costly optional war we waged in Vietnam. Despite these costs, America became the world's richest and most powerful country in the world. We reached this enviable position because of our hard work, "can do" attitude, a sense of optimism and the combination of advantages our nation enjoyed including demographic, geographic, political, economic and social.

However, in the 1980's in the name of globalization our government drove our manufacturing industry overseas by imposing a high corporate tax structure on the profits they made in the U.S. Corporate greed was also a factor in this exodus. As a result our skilled jobs were hollowed out and our middle class was decimated. We were beginning to face a crisis of economic inequality before the pandemic hit us.

Don't let the COVID-19 Crisis go to Waste

To address this pandemic, Congress passed the largest economic stimulus package in American history to protect our workers from wages lost due to unemployment and businesses from bankruptcies. What is needed now is an honest self-appraisal of the problems we are facing as a country and find serious and lasting solutions.

Our corporate tax structure has been improved recently for doing business on our soil. Additional economic stimulus to help our industries is in the works. We should apply the lessons learnt from our economic history to rebuild America.

We need innovative thinking befitting the 21st Century to reindustrialize our country by embracing new technologies. Technologies such as artificial intelligence, robotics, zero-emission automobiles and remote learning should be harnessed to rebuild. We should we willing to apply the proven economic models of other countries such as Canada, Finland and Western Europe in medicines, healthcare and education to wisely invest and improve the lives of our citizenry.

The renewal of America is not limited to reinventing, but by returning to our values that once made us singular. We should do more to invest in our country's infrastructure, reduce consumption, limit the size of our bureaucracies while strengthening our institutions, lessen entitlements and avoid costly optional wars. Importantly, we should preserve the rule of law, enshrine meritocracy and inculcate national pride in our old customs and traditions while ensuring liberty, freedom and equality of our citizens. Such a plan will lead us back to the pursuit of happiness.

30

COMPROMISE WILL REUNIFY AMERICA

Published in Las Vegas Sun *on August 8, 2020*

AMERICA IS A unique and admirable country which every American is proud of. America did not become the world's richest and most powerful country by accident. We reached this singular position because we carry a sense of optimism and have a "can-do" attitude. Other strengths contributed to our status including a demography of relatively young population, a geography protected by the Pacific and Atlantic oceans on two sides and friendly neighbors on the other sides, a political system of democracy based on three branches of government, an economic system founded on capitalism, a rich history of struggle and success, and the rule of law.

America fought national and international wars. We transformed Germany and Japan from vanquished enemies of World War II into trusted and prosperous allies. After this War we won the Cold War against the Russians. We were generous with our prosperity and strength and helped many countries around the world to lift them out of poverty and suppression. We became a beacon of hope for humanity and a role model for the world.

American power, however, is fragile. The advantages we

enjoy as a nation can be easily squandered. Ominous signs of such squander are beginning to emerge. High among the warning signs is the erosion of our system of democracy which historically has been a pillar of strength. Another warning sign is the attempt to chip away our economic capitalism which perennially bore fruit.

We are facing an accelerating deterioration of political compromise in our democracy. Without compromise democracy will deteriorate to tyranny. It is the breakdown of compromise that led to our 1861-1865 Civil War.

Political polarization is the most dangerous problem America is facing now. It is more dangerous than the competition from China, illegal immigration from Mexico or the coronavirus epidemic.

Compromise between our Democratic and Republican Parties has been deteriorating since about 2008 and has been progressively getting worse. The problem started within the Republican Party when a rift arose between the factions of extreme right wing Tea Party and the moderate wing. Likewise, within the Democratic Party the more extreme liberals are dominating at the expense of the middle-of-the-roaders.

The extremists in both parties got elected because of election campaign contributions from the Wall Street and other rich entities and individuals who influence the government policy to suit their needs. This invisible form of corruption that is embedded in our elections and lobbying in Congress is unfortunately becoming an accepted norm and no one is able to clean it up.

As expected, the extremists have taken control over their party and are influencing their leaders with their ideals and have driven them to the edges. They seem to have forgotten that American people are flexible as individuals and expect their elected leaders to acknowledge the other party's views and reach a compromise.

The opportunity to compromise was the centerpiece of governing when Ronald Reagan was the President when, despite divergent political views, he worked closely with the Democratic Speaker of the House Tip O'Neill, by giving something in return for something else and got legislation passed. Our present counterparts of these leaders should emulate their behavior.

Congress as an institution should compel a return to compromise and accommodation. Human dignity also demands compromise. We need a good civil debate among members of Congress who have opposing views and adapt to give and take as a way to compromise.

America is at a crossroad now. We should be talking about our future. How to mitigate death and disease and save our economy from the pandemic? How to educate our children during the pandemic? How to bring about social order? How to address the police and race? How to manage social media which have eroded the value of our institutions?

How to ensure our ideals of equality, unity and individual liberty are safeguarded? How should America be positioned in the 2050's and beyond?

The move to erode our economic capitalism and replace it with socialism should be debated. Capitalism worked for America since the time of our country's birth. It made us the richest country. Even totalitarian countries like China having tasted capitalism are now wedded to it. We should have a debate on income inequality under our capitalism where the average income of an American CEO is 40 times the income of the average worker and find a solution to alleviate this disparity.

Socialism has a dark history of failure and wrought misery to countries that practiced this economic model. It is contrary to the principle of democracy and free enterprise that made our nation prosperous.

Americans demand pragmatic solutions to these and other problems setting aside the ideology of left as well as right through compromise and mutual respect for the bedrock of ideologies. Such pragmatism should be grounded on realistic, moral, and ethical values. We need a united America to collectively solve our nation's problems.

31

QUANTUM INTERNET AND ITS BIG BROTHER

Published as a post in LinkedIn on August 16, 2020

IT IS AMERICAN ingenuity with tax-payer funding by the U.S. Department of Defense that led to the creation of the first ever internet communication in 1969. It was then known as the ARPANET.

The claim made in 1999 by U.S. Vice President Al Gore that "he took the initiative in creating the internet" was mistakenly interpreted that he was the inventor of the internet. No one person can be credited as the inventor of the internet. The internet was a collective national effort.

The internet is an indispensable part of our daily communication through email. We share personal messages, family photographs, music, videos and everything under the sun that was previously shared via physical media can now be shared digitally using the internet.

Internet usage soared substantially during the coronavirus pandemic because millions of Americans had to rely on their home internet to work, learn, communicate and entertain themselves.

The internet has expanded to link nearly every country on Earth. Even some of the poorest countries are now connected. In 2006 the internet has been named by *USA Today* as a human-built Wonder of the World.

How does the internet work? Simply, the internet is a network of computers which moves information (data) from one computer (the sender) to another (the receiver). Most data, for example an email, moves in the form of tiny pieces called packets where each packet is tagged with a protocol, its originating and destination addresses and a packet number and allowed to travel separately by different routes. The packets are transmitted via underground fiber-optic or copper cables or over wireless communication through space. When the packets reach their destination, the packets are reassembled into their original format and reconverted into the original email.

The internet is aided by routers which make connection between different computers on the network and servers constituting the cloud which store data for retrieval when needed.

The internet revitalized our commercial use starting in the1990's. It is now routinely used to transmit information related to national security, health, business, and financial, governmental and other services. When confidentiality of data is needed it is encrypted during transmission which requires secret keys to decrypt.

Hacking of the internet by rogue individuals and nations has become a common place now. Individuals hack to extract money from the data owners and internet service providers. Rogue nations like China, Iran, North Korea and Russia attempt to infiltrate our internet infrastructure of under-ground and underwater fiber cables and satellite communication vehicles. With cyber-attacks they attempt to disrupt our energy grids, military and missile launch sites, food and water supply chains, financial and national voting systems, etc. which are linked via the internet. They also attempt to steal sensitive information from leading American defense companies and pose a real problem to our national security. The hackers found ways to even thwart encrypted data.

An effort is underway in the U.S. to build the nation's second internet which among other benefits will be the gold standard for data security. The U.S. Department of Energy is leading the development of this new communications network called the quantum internet. This project is funded in part by the $1.275 billion budget allocated as part of President Trump's National Quantum Initiative.

The DOE and the University of Chicago and more than 50 public and private organizations are involved in developing the U.S.-based quantum internet by competing with Canada and other countries. In the private sector IBM and Google in the U.S. and Rigetti Computing in Canada are investing heavily in quantum computing technology.

Current computers manipulate packets which store information. Quantum computers leverage the strange quantum mechanical properties of superposition and entanglement to manipulate information.

Superposition is a phenomenon where a quantum system

can exist in multiple states or places at the same time. Entanglement is the strong correlation that exists between two or more quantum particles. Under quantum entanglement, if you observe a particle in one place, another particle–even light-years away–will instantly change its properties, as if the two are connected by a mysterious communication channel. Physicists have observed entanglement in atoms and electrons.

Albert Einstein colorfully derided quantum entanglement as "spooky action at a distance", but physicists have demonstrated the reality of the spooky action at unprecedented distances from Earth to satellites in space.

Quantum internet experiments are now underway. Scientists from DOE and the University of Chicago in February stated that they had established a quantum network of 52 miles worth of entangled photons running on unused telecom fiber-optic cables in the Chicago suburbs.

Creating entangled photons and keeping them entangled while information is being conveyed across long distances is a challenge for physicists in creating the quantum internet. One way of creating entangled photons is to use nonlinear optical crystals that, when excited by a pulse of light, can create a pair of entangled photons according to David Awschalom of the University of Chicago.

Scientists are experimenting with sophisticated devices called quantum repeaters - equipped with quantum memory modules–placed along the nodes of the quantum internet. The repeaters receive photons from two different places, then store them in quantum memory and make sure that they remain entangled before sending further as information over the internet.

There are many challenges facing the quantum repeaters as they are complex systems requiring complex quantum and conventional devices to function at the highest performance levels. Nevertheless, progress is being made in recent years with new approaches.

Building a scalable quantum memory device which in the past functioned at near absolute zero to operate at room temperature is now a reality at IBM. Likewise sophisticated quantum processors are under development to process data (known as quantum bits) employed in the quantum transmission.

IBM and Google are in a race to achieve supremacy in quantum computers by using the resources of entanglement and superposition in unique ways. No matter which company attains this supremacy, quantum computers will fundamentally change the landscape of information technology.

One of the hallmarks of quantum transmission is that they are exceedingly difficult to eavesdrop on the information (e.g., email) that passes between locations. If a hacker tried to intercept the email encoded in the entangled photons at any time during transmission, the properties of the photons would be disturbed and the entanglement would be broken. The email would appear scrambled to the hacker and also arrive scrambled to the person receiving it.

This trait will make the quantum internet virtually un-hackable without breaking the laws of physics.

Quantum internet will be game-changing for every industry. It will have a much more profound impact on the way we do business, invent new materials and medicines, and protect our sensitive data transmitted over the new internet more securely than ever before.

Like the ARPANET no one person can claim to be the inventor of the quantum internet. It is a collective national or perhaps an international effort that is driving its creation. The quantum internet is expected to be fully functional before the end of this decade.

BIG BROTHER INTERNET
Paradoxically, for all the benefits that internet brought to life, it gave rise to the new age of surveillance of citizens like George Orwell envisioned in his 1949 novel titled *1984*. As feared by Orwell, totalitarian governments are now the Big Brother. They monitor their citizens by using the internet as a convenient surveillance tool for suppression and tyranny. They use the internet to spread disinformation at home and abroad.

Democratic governments are less prone to be the Big Brother. However, the big titans of technology in the

Silicon Valley are using technology coupled with access to the internet for redefining the way internet users live and the freedom they enjoy. They endlessly intrude into the private life of users to sell goods and services to them and track their shopping, viewing and reading habits. Such user data has become highly profitable and is being exploited for commercial gain.

These titans have the capability to track their users' physical movements as well as their private messaging. So far, they resisted to handover such tracking data and messaging to the government except when criminal activity was involved.

However, the dangers exist that the titans, particularly those dominating the social media, could become the de-facto Big Brother. They could turn the internet as a propaganda tool to suit their interests and violate the user's Constitutional rights if the government fails to intervene.

PART II

AFTER WRITING

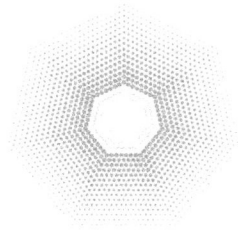

A MAN'S PURPOSE is only known to God. I believe in God. I continue to search what God intended me to be. The answer remains elusive.

I am a man of the world. Born in the rich cultural and vibrant Indian subcontinent where I was raised until I reached 22. For the rest of my life of well over half century I lived in the United States. I managed not to be planted in one place in my adopted country. I embraced change rather than denying it which led me to greater and unknown opportunities and a better understanding of the world that I never imagined.

By choice I moved around and lived in over a dozen towns and cities across the United States from the East to mid-West and the West, all of which enhanced my personal and professional life.

While being domiciled in America, I was fortunate to have lived for half a decade in Tokyo, Japan by virtue of my posting in the Asia-Pacific region. My posting encompassed the countries of Australia, China, Hong Kong, India, Indonesia, Japan, Malaysia, New Zealand, Philippines, Singapore, South Korea, Taiwan, and Vietnam.

Travel is in my blood. Friends call me a gypsy. This is somewhat a derogatory characterization. I prefer to call myself a world traveler.

Besides travelling to take care of business, I travelled on my own to experience the geographical terrain and climate naturally formed on our planet. I travelled to be educated by a mosaic of wonders of diverse architecture, history, religions, culture, monuments, languages and food that were created by humans.

I was fortunate to have travelled around the world–I mean literally circled the world–six times. I was enriched by being in all of the continents on the Earth, perhaps missing a couple of places like Iceland and Greenland, which continue to be on my bucket list.

Gaining worldly education by traveling has been a component of my overall knowledge. I was lucky to have been formally educated not in a single discipline but in multiple; not in a single country but in two.

Formal education in physics, mathematics and chemistry combined with multiple languages laid the foundation to my early schooling in India. After earning my bachelors' degree in physics, mathematics and chemistry, I settled into a study of physics and was trained as a physicist through advanced and scholarly studies at universities.

If academic degrees are a measure of one's stature in education, I earned a bachelor's degree in physics and mathematics, a master's degree in nuclear physics, another master's in optical physics and a doctorate in solid state physics. Two of these degrees were earned from a university in India and the other two from a university in America.

My life did not always go the way I expected it will. My yearning to pursue career as a physicist did not materialize right away. The four degrees I earned was not the inflexion point of my formal education. Circumstances beyond my control altered my career trajectory in an unexpected way. They veered me to the university again to pursue more studies, this time in law. After four years of study I earned the degree of Juris Doctor to be eligible to be licensed as an American lawyer.

Passing bar examinations and getting admitted to the states of Ohio, New York and Vermont, the United States Patent and Trademark Office, the Court of Appeals for the Federal Circuit and the Supreme Court of the United States were my crowning accomplishments.

The doors that were shut to me right after I earned my doctorate seem to immediately open after I became an American lawyer. Overall my professional life was a thrilling run.

I practiced as a corporate lawyer specializing in Intellectual Property for over four decades. I married my physics background with law to join this specialty which is recognized by the American Bar Association after satisfying additional bar requirements.

Before settling into law, for a short period I had the pleasure of working as a physicist and later as a software designer in the aerospace company of General Dynamics Corporation in San Diego, CA. Before that, I imparted knowledge of physics to eager and wide-eyed students at the high school, college and university levels in the suburbs of Philadelphia, PA.

My years of upbringing in India, living across the vast continental United States as well as in Asia Pacific shaped me to be what I am now. The culture, economics, and geopolitics of these diverse regions coalesced into my multifaceted thinking and accommodation. New career experiences around the world made me grow with the richness of knowledge gained from them.

Although I initially trained to be a physicist I took a liking to politics. Politics at the domestic and international level fascinated me. At first I only had a superficial understanding of it. Even though I never experienced the threats of fascism or communism when I grew up in India, democracy is what I am accustomed to and it is deeply ingrained in me.

I could have gone for advanced studies to communist Russia or the newly liberated Nazi Germany where a part of the City of Berlin was still under control by Russia. I chose not to. The beacon of hope that America has been beckoned me in the 1960's with its democratic principles of freedom of thought, speech, religion, rule of law and association. I arrived in America in 1965 and remained here ever since.

I am now awakened to the conservative way of thinking on most issues. However, when first arrived in the U.S. I innocently rooted for the leaders of the Democratic Party without discerning the differences between the two opposing parties of our democratic system of government. I admired the charisma and speeches of John F. Kennedy as a President before I arrived here. That admiration initially moved me to vote for the democrats after I earned my privilege to vote.

I realized such admiration and voting was ill-founded because I was then not fully exposed to the American history and did not know the truth of what each of the political parties really stood for.

As I gradually assimilated into the American society my political philosophy was awakened. Reading books on American history and politics was eye-opening and broadened my view of America. By observing the politics in action and the liberal pundits of academia in my graduate school and the two law schools I attended and the one-sided views of the dominant newspapers like the New York Times, Washington Post and Los Angeles Times and the television media like CNN and MSNBC, I gradually developed an aversion to their left-leaning viewpoints.

I veered toward centrist thinking on most issues. Moderation became my watchword, as opposed to taking extreme positions advocated by the left as well as the right. When the left moved toward the extreme, I shifted to the right. As I moved around the United States from Pennsylvania, to California, Ohio, New York, Vermont, Connecticut and Nevada and resided in them my voter registration covered the spectrum of Democratic, Republican and Independent affiliations. Now, I characterize myself as a center-right Republican.

I believe in a government that serves our middle class

first and the Washington establishment last. I believe in a limited government that provides essential and necessary social services and manages itself with fiscal restraint and responsibility. I believe in a strong military to protect our nation from enemies, but not engage in optional wars abroad.

Having put myself through the rigors of the U.S. Immigration System, I take pride in qualifying as a foreigner for my student visa which enabled me to legally enter the United States. This was followed by qualifying, based solely on skills and scholarship, for my permanent residency in the U.S. (or Green Card). Five years later I celebrated when I earned my American citizenship through naturalization.

I believe in America with secure borders and enforcement of our immigration laws which have been the most generous in the world for foreigners to come legally and live in America. Sovereignty requires secure borders. As an American citizen and particularly as an American lawyer I believe in the rule of law. Violation of our immigration laws is abhorrent to me.

I reached a fulcrum point in my world political view of America after I returned in 1995 from my five year international assignment in Japan. During my time abroad I worked as a lawyer representing the IBM Corporation. In that capacity I cooperated and harmonized on public policy matters with the U.S. State Department and negotiated deals for IBM with public and private entities in a dozen countries in Asia-Pacific. I developed an increasing understanding of how the foreign governments were taking advantage of us as we embarked on globalization.

More than any other country in the Asia-Pacific region, China was the most egregious culprit. I began to realize how the Chinese Communist Party was monitoring the movement of American visitors to their country.

Counterfeits of American products were being sold in open markets all over in China, Hong Kong and Taiwan (which China claimed as the Greater China). Personal computers, printers, software packages, compact discs of music and newly released Hollywood movies and even designer clothing by affixing fake brand names on them was rampant. Registration of trademarks and patents did not deter them from this lucrative copycat business.

The authorities did not discourage them from such trade. Some officials from the ruling Chinese Communist Party were known to be driving this illicit trade and became oligarchs.

Also, China's pernicious habit of infiltrating the U.S. private sector and government research laboratories through espionage and stealing our industrial secrets and intellectual property became apparent.

China's ultimate goal became obvious to me in the early 90's. China wanted to amass wealth to modernize its infrastructure. Nothing came in the way to raise wealth. Beg, borrow and steal were the tools China used. China also wished to accelerate its rebuilding. Stealing was a fast, convenient and easily available way. China readily engaged in such activity against the U.S. which had the best of the technology for rebuilding. Because of this China was able to leap-frog years of time and save billions of dollars that America invested to create its technology, intellectual property and confidential manufacturing and industrial know-how.

It later dawned on me then that the ultimate goal of China has all along been to dominate the world with an unrelenting grip of totalitarianism held by its ruling Communist Party.

In my travels I discovered that the Chinese people seem to be present everywhere on the earth including on some remote island nations. Everywhere they settled they set up shop invariably in the form of a Chinese restaurant, laundry service or a mom and pop store where they sold shoddy products imported from China. My discussions with the locals in the large established country like Australia and the tiny islands of Trinidad and Tobago alike reinforced that the Chinese were tight with their money. The locals detested them for their parsimoniousness, aloofness and failing to build relationships with their customers.

When China entered a foreign country to build infra-structure projects like airports or public housing, China ensured that a binding and enforceable contract for lending is established with the local bodies. China's motivation for funding such projects is to secure access to the local markets. As a result borrower countries like Sri Lanka are now hugely in debt to China.

The *Wall Street Journal* recently reported that China is now hurriedly collecting more than $200 billion from overseas lending. Despite being the second largest economy in the world China is not known to extend free aid to foreign countries no matter how poor and desperate such countries are.

Endowed with a strong foundation of broad and diverse education and over fifty years of national and international experience in diverse avocations as a teacher, physicist, software architect, Intellectual Property lawyer, manager, mentor, speaker and writer, I finally settled to write following my retirement.

Writing has been my passion. Writing takes all of the creative juices to use as well as precious time. I have a limited amount of them as they competed with my need to share my skills and experiences with others in the society. I wrote thirty one articles during the period of 2013 to 2020.

I compiled these writings in Part I of this book.

To practice the art of writing I emulated what a graduate student would to fulfil the requirement of a thesis to earn an advanced university degree. Having earned my Ph. D. degree I was intimately familiar with the process. It entailed: select a topic of interest to the readers; conduct research on it to understand what has been written; identify an issue to tackle which is consequential to the topic; explain the topic's background and present my solution to the issue, and package it through logical and succinct writing which would be accepted by the reader.

While my writings in this compilation seem like a hodge-podge, there is a common thread that links them. The thread is simply the issues I wrestled with in my life and on which I developed some expertise. I saw issues that other people didn't and I felt compelled to throw the spotlight on them. I wanted to share my views with others through these writings.

This common thread stretches across topics in Education, Innovation, Work, Immigration, Trade, and finally on the ever-changing trade and economic relationship between America and China.

The latter relationship now plummeted to the level of an economic Cold War. I strongly feel about this deteriorating relationship.

Let me attempt to bring the 'semblance of connection among these seven topics.

EDUCATION: WRITINGS 1, 2, 19, AND 21

IN THE FIRST two writings, having observed first hand and up close as to what was happening in our higher education system at the University of Nevada in Las Vegas and by direct communication with the Nevada Governor's Office of Economic Development, I lay out the need to capitalize on the intellectual property owned by these institutions.

I describe my obsession to turn intellectual property owned by our universities into sustainable revenue. With decades of experience in the corporate world where my teams monetized patents and generated billions of dollars of income for IBM, I advocated to adopt this model to public institutions like the Nevada GOED and UNLV.

I also advocate that every faculty member is capable of monetizing their intellect through invention and creative writings to raise cash. I boldly state that *"perhaps the faculty tenure process should be modified to make commercialization of their intellectual capabilities a factor."*

Likewise, universities who are sitting on patents and other non-tangible intellectual property assets can license or divest them to raise cash. Such cash when contributed to the finances of the university the burden of tuition that students are forced to pay is alleviated.

In a subsequent writing (19), I advocate the immediate

need to educate our high school graduates in a 2-year apprenticeship rather than a 4-year university degree program with skills in science, technology, engineering and math that our employers are craving for. I saw this need as dire in Nevada where the STEM education has taken a back seat.

I wrote that apprenticeships have been around for hundreds of years. Specifically, I wrote *"vocational technical programs in technology have been highly successful in industrialized countries like Germany, China and India. These countries decades ago realized the value of training in STEM and heavily invested in meeting such need for their country. They immensely benefitted from such investment."*

In the same article I point out the under representation of females in STEM subjects and attribute this shortage to the schools' guidance counsellors and parents who acquiesce in letting the female students pick the path of least resistance, namely a non-STEM major.

I wrote that apprenticeships should be set up as a public - private partnership to be successful where an employer works as a training partner with community colleges and non-profit community-based organizations. Such employer-led training will impart baseline knowledge and skills as well as customized training that jobs require. Apprenticeships will also remove barrier to entry by opening up workers without college degrees.

Such advocacy in education became my campaign platform when I ran for election to serve as a regent of the

Nevada State Board of Regents in 2018. In my writing 21 ("Running for Election of Board of Regents in Nevada") I elaborated my background in education and career and life experiences and bared my reasons to run for this voluntary position. This was my first attempt to run for a political office. I wanted to be a voice of reason to correct the dismal shape of education in the state under the direction of the Nevada System of Higher Education.

INNOVATION: WRITINGS 5, 8, 9, 11, 12, 14, AND 31

IN THIS SERIES of articles, which I wrote over a span of six years, I felt compelled to inform the readers how our country has been a leader in innovation of new technologies; and how to safeguard such technologies which were created by investing billions of dollars and a vast human intellectual capital. I have seen how IBM tracked inventions made by its scientists and engineers and protected them by secrecy and through patents. I personally take pride in helping IBM earn its status as the top ranked U.S. patentee for decades as I was instrumental in achieving that sustained and unique rank during my tenure at this company.

Some of these articles reflect my paranoia that when the valuable intellectual property asset if left unprotected, it may fall in the hands of our adversaries who are constantly looking to steal it because of our inadvertence or by their covert espionage. Intellectual property is time sensitive upon its creation. I throw precautionary tales to small and large businesses alike that intellectual property is like fresh fruit which needs to be timely protected or else it will perish.

In this batch, I also write (in article 8, "Europe's Inability to Compete") how Europe lost its way in innovation from its past glorious years during the Renaissance period in the

19th and early 20th Centuries. I attribute it to the never-ending regulations imposed by the local governments which stifled and eventually killed off the spark of creativity and the human spirit to innovate. Having lost the power to innovate, the European Union now resorted to punishing innovating American companies. It is well known that by applying Europe's narrowly written anti-trust laws against IBM, Intel, Microsoft, Google, Apple, Qualcomm, Facebook and others EU unfairly collected tens of billions of dollars of fines from them.

Finally, in article 32 ("Quantum Internet and its Big Brother") I went back to my roots as a physicist, dating back to nearly fifty years, and attempted to describe in layman terms the new invention of quantum internet which is under development at the U.S. Department of Energy by collaborating with University of Chicago. The quantum internet among other benefits is a gold standard for data security communicated through this network. However, we will have to wait for a decade for it to be a reality.

In this article I point out how our technology titans in the Silicon Valley are now using the internet, as feared by George Orwell in his novel *1984*. Some of these titans are tracking the physical locations of their users and also monitoring their communications over the internet like the Big Brother portrayed in Orwell's book. They have become behemoths with a market capitalization of a trillion dollars or more by using users' behavioral data and selling products and services to them.

Yet, these titans refuse to cooperate with our government to track terrorists and criminals who operate by using internet services they provide. They refuse to be patriotic or keep America safe from domestic and foreign enemies.

Relevant to this unpatriotic behavior are the remarks by Alex Karp who is the co-founder and CEO of Palantir, a firm based in Palo Alto, CA that recently relocated to Denver, CO. Palantir is a Big Data company that serves the automobile manufacturing industry as well as the U.S. defense and intelligence agencies.

Alex chides the elite Silicon Valley titans of their increasing intolerance and mono-culture and warns: *"Americans will remain tolerant of the idiosyncrasies and excesses of the Valley only to the extent that technology companies are building something substantial that serves the public interest. The corporate form itself—that is, the privilege to engage in private enterprise—is a product of the state and would not exist without it."*

Alex distinguishes his company for patriotic duty from the Valley titans this way: *"Our software is used to target terrorists and to keep soldiers safe. If we are going to ask someone to put themselves in harm's way, we believe that we have a duty to give them what they need to do their job. We have chosen sides, and we know that our partners value our commitment. We stand by them when it is convenient, and when it is not."*

Washington-based Amazon.com, another titan operating its business on the internet is truly a Big Brother. Amazon uses such tools as navigation software, item scanners, wristbands, thermal cameras and recorded footage to surveil its workforce in warehouses and stores. This invasive form of surveillance is intended to boost employees' output and potentially limit unionization efforts. Such surveillance, however, is prohibited by the U.S. Department of Labor; and so far no known action has been taken against Amazon.

WORK: WRITINGS 3, 10, 20, 23, 27, AND 28

IN THIS ENSEMBLE of writings on work, I ardently hammer that our multinational companies have an obligation to bring back the U.S. jobs that they exported to countries like China to take advantage of the cheap labor available there. In article 10 ("Corporations have Legal, Ethical and Economic Responsibilities") I castigate these companies for failing to show their loyalty and social responsibility to the country in which they are incorporated. I decry that instead they hollowed out our muscle states of Pennsylvania, Ohio, Michigan, Wisconsin, and others of industrial jobs. They were driven by greed to generate more profits from their overseas operations at the expense of U.S. workers.

In my article 3 ("How to Bring Jobs Back to U.S.") which I wrote in 2014, I propose a methodology to bring back as many as 300,000 U.S. jobs per year which companies offshored since the Great Recession of 2007 to foreign countries like China, India, Mexico because of cheap labor available there. I proposed an incentive plan to bring back those jobs by lowering the federal corporate tax rate from 39.1% to about 20%. In addition, I proposed a conditional tax holiday when the trillions of dollars of profits made overseas are repatriated to our country. The condition was that in return for tax-free repatriation the companies should agree to reinvest that money to build research, development and manufacturing centers and create high-paying jobs in the U.S.

In two articles in this ensemble ("It is time for Companies to Bring Jobs Home", written in 2018 and "America Benefits by Bringing Businesses Home", written in 2020) I applaud the green shoots that were beginning to emerge across our nation in terms of our multinational companies slowly returning to our land. This return and investment in our communities was prompted by the 2017 Federal Tax Cuts and Jobs Act which slashed our corporate tax from 39% to 21%. The TCJA also permitted repatriation of profits earned overseas at a lower tax rate. This is spurring trillions of cash parked overseas to return to the U.S. for creating new jobs here.

Coincidentally, the drafters of TCJA seem to have followed at least parts of the suggestions I made in my April 2014 writing #3 (on "How to Bring Jobs Back to the U.S.") which are now codified into law in 2017.

Despite the attractive tax incentives offered by our government some U.S. multinationals are not doing their fair share in bringing jobs back to our shores. The most egregious of such multinationals is IBM which shifted its center of gravity halfway around the world to India. The New York Times reported in 2018 that out of IBM's overall workforce of 380,000 the company employs 130,000 people in India. So much so, the acronym for IBM is now dubbed as India Business Machines! Likewise, Oracle Corporation reportedly has 130,000 worldwide jobs of which 40,000 jobs are in India.

Dell.com has 25,000 jobs based in India, out of 138,000 jobs worldwide.

All of these U.S. multinationals are software powerhouses and established their subsidiary companies in India to take advantage of the software skills that the Indian programmers possess. However, software skills particularly coding can be easily taught to American workers who do not have a foundation in STEM. Stories have been published that students who majored in liberal arts like music have picked up skills in software coding after a short period of concentrated on-the-job training.

Our multinationals receive a huge cost benefit by employing workers in foreign countries to develop cutting-edge research, managing advanced software development and coding. They need to reach a balance in creating an excessive number of skilled jobs overseas versus jobs in America. They need to show their social and moral responsibility to the citizens of America where their company was incorporated and received the benefits associated with such incorporation.

In Article 20 titled "Baby Boomers Experience and Skills is a Terrible Thing to Waste" I extoll the enormous skills and experience that our country's baby boomers have amassed over their lifetime of nearly five or more decades. They are now nearing retirement or affected by mass layoffs amid the coronavirus pandemic. I urge our private sector and educational institutions to have their knowledge and experience transferred to our country's younger generation and avoid creating a generational gap in their staff.

If the baby boomers do not transfer their skills, there might be a historic plunge in many critical U.S. industries. For example, in the Oil and Gas Industry, which offers good paying jobs, the employed baby boomers have garnered special skills and amazing talents. Their collective experience will be a waste if it is not transferred to rebuild fresh talent in this industry.

Our employers should recruit fresh talent, build teams by using the baby boomers as scouts. It is best to rehire the retired boomers as consultants and establish 3-6-month internships to train fresh talent of students and new graduates who are passionate about getting trained for good jobs. By using the boomers' creativity and experience to train this new workforce, our employers would bring a quick rebound of our job market.

IMMIGRATION: WRITINGS 6, 13 AND 15

I PUT MYSELF through the U.S. Immigration System and know how it works. Before I turned 22, I filled out the paperwork, furnished the supporting documentation required by our Immigration & Naturalization Service, and subjected myself for an interview by the U.S. Consulate in Madras, India to earn my student visa. This visa enabled me enter America, Following this as a doctoral student, based on my skill and scholarship I qualified under the Fifth Preference category of the U.S. Immigration & Nationality Act of 1965 for my permanent residency (the Green Card) in the U.S. I endured the application process, the rigors of Immigration's personal interviews and a medical examination by the Immigration doctors and earned my Green Card. The Green Card is a life's lottery of inestimable value!

After meeting a five year residency in the U.S. and demonstrating that I did not have any criminal record and that I did not commit any act of moral turpitude and passing tests in the proficiency in the English language and in the history of our government and how it works, I eventually earned my U.S. citizenship.

Later, by sponsoring members of my core and extended foreign-born family for immigration to America, I became adept on the subject of immigration. The courses I took on immigration law in law school, my initial thought of practicing immigration law after earning my JD and my immense interest in the story of immigration enabled me to develop an understanding of our country's immigration laws.

The valuable lessons I learned by subjecting myself to the U.S. Immigration & Naturalization system, I developed admiration for the lawful immigration process and how thorough and effective it has been. Overall, I cherish the generosity of the American people to have given me an opportunity to lawfully come to America and build my life through immigration.

My firm belief that a country's sovereignty dictates strict and total control of its borders comes through in these writings. This is a bedrock belief that I hold.

I strongly believe in legal immigration to the U.S. but disfavor illegal immigration. Illegal immigration from our southern border has been taking place for over five decades. No U.S. President starting from Lyndon Johnson took action to stop it until President Donald Trump was elected in 2016. He initiated strong measures to curb it.

I believe that our Immigration Nationality Act of 1965 is outdated. The 1965 INA served its purpose at the time it was enacted. Since then piecemeal amendments were made to this Act over time. However, a rewrite of this law is needed by the U.S. Congress to bring the immigration law to conform to our needs of the 21st Century.

Our asylum system for refugees is broken; so are chain

migration and the sale of our Greed Cards under the guise of EB-5 visa program mostly to rich foreigners like the Chinese. In my writing 13 ("Reform of U.S. Immigration Laws Needed") I propose specific measures of reform that is needed of our existing immigration laws.

I also suggest that America should import immigrants when there is a shortage of skilled labor and when a need arises to fill vacant jobs under a temporary work permit. In the past, the immigrants who studied in our universities and received advanced degrees made outsized contribution to the U.S. economy through innovation.

I propose that the nearly 300,000 foreign students that annually graduate from our universities with advanced degrees should be incented to remain in the U.S. if they possess the skills and talent our country is in need of. Offering them the permanent resident status would be a lucrative incentive. By offering them the Green Card they remain here and continue to contribute to American innovation, entrepreneurism and overall good of our society. They may eventually become citizens and add to our gene pool.

However, for political reasons a rewrite or reform of our immigration law is unlikely to happen as along as the Democratic Party holds a majority in our House of Representatives. The Democrats want to continue the present status quo on our southern border which allows every year of millions of aliens from Mexico and other Latin American countries to infiltrate into our country. The Democratic Party manages to manipulate such illegals and makes possible for such noncitizens to illegally vote for their party in congressional elections.

The Democratic Party continues to harbor the illegal aliens in the District of Columbia and in many states including California, Oregon, Washington, Minnesota, Illinois, New York, Massachusetts, and others by transforming them into sanctuary districts and states. The Democrats manages to incent the illegals by offering government-sponsored health and unemployment benefits and guarantees safety and security which are reserved for U.S. citizens while not educating the illegals to pay the city, state and federal taxes on the income they earn clandestinely.

The race of the American people is a driving factor for the Democratic Party in everything it does. The white voters have slowly and consistently moved away from the Democratic Party because the Party decades ago abandoned them. The last time the Democratic Party received a majority of white votes in a Presidential election is over eighty years ago dating back to the year when Franklin Roosevelt won. In the last five presidential elections Bill Clinton received 49% of the white vote in 1996, Gore received 43% in 2000, John Kerry received 41% in 2004, and Obama received only 39% in 2012, according to the Washington Post.

As a result, the Democratic Party has been consistently courting non-whites regardless of whether they are in the U.S. legally or illegally and persuades them to vote for their party in return for overlooking the illegal status of many. This has been an on-going process that the Democratic Party adopted for the very survival of their party.

Actually the Democratic Party first tried a similar approach and succeeded with its plantation mentality to coerce black Americans who worked as slaves in the cotton fields and other plantations in the south to vote for their party. The plantation mentality of the Southern Democrats gradually spread to the Northern Democrats and alienated the white voters. Now the Democratic Party is preying upon illegal aliens under their slogan of "open borders" and ignoring the sacred sovereignty of our country.

Sadly, a rewrite of our immigration laws will happen only when the House is taken over by a Republican majority.

TRADE: WRITINGS 17, 18 AND 22

THE TRADE FRICTION that broke up in 2018 when President Trump took action by imposing tariffs on goods imported from China in retaliation for the high tariffs that China imposed on imported American goods has been long overdue. Every U.S. President from starting from Richard Nixon overlooked China's behavior on trade which was atrocious. China manipulated the world when it joined the World Trade Organization in 2001 by labeling itself as a developing country to avoid paying tariffs on goods it exported overseas, but applied heavy tariffs on goods it imported.

The drama created by the trade tariffs motivated me to write a series of articles to explain why the Chinese tariffs are costing American jobs and the extent to which our economy is suffering and adding to our deficits.

In article 22 on stealing of the U.S. intellectual property and trade tariffs I described the systematic and deliberate way in which China practiced forced technology transfer from American companies who wanted to do business there in these terms:

"China's theft of U.S. IP is wanton, deliberate and coerced and has been going on for more than three decades and continues now despite China's present status as the second largest economy behind the U.S.

It was wanton, because when China opened up its econo-my to foreign investment in the late 1980's, following protests by students to democratize the country, it did not have any IP of its own to depend on. China was impatient to invest and create its own IP as pressure from its people for quick political reform mounted. The government needed to engage in Western-style industrialization in a hurry. Stealing of IP was an easy way out.

The theft was deliberate because the government engaged its state agencies and military personnel to snoop into our open business enterprises and walked away with a valuable loot of stolen IP which they used to produce products in competition with our companies.

The theft was coerced for several reasons. China fore-stalled legal protection for IP that U.S. companies sought from China Intellectual Property Office since it did not want the U.S. companies to have a lock on such IP. Second, the Chinese government then imposed an arbitrary rule upon foreign companies who wanted to do business in China: the foreign company must establish a 50/50 joint venture with a Chinese partner. Invariably, the Chinese partner was comprised of camouflaged military group. In fact, China controlled the workers that the JV needed. The modus operandi used for the JV to hire employees was this. A roster of personnel was offered to the foreign partner to select from. Some in this roster were spies selected by the Chinese government to steal the technology that the foreign partner possessed or *transferred into the JV. In other words, the JV was a conduit for siphoning off the IP of the foreign partner.*

There was one other way a U.S. entity could do business in China. This was the conventional way of exporting products made in the U.S. into China, but those products were subjected to high Chinese tariffs."

In this connection I offered eight specific suggestions on how to solve this problem with IP theft and end the trade tariffs.

Before President Trump was leaning toward walking away from multilateral agreements that U.S. signed like the World Trade Organization treaty in lieu of a bilateral agreement with China, I felt compelled to research the historical lessons learned from these types of agreements that America signed and how well they are working. The upshot (which I discussed in writing 17) was that bilateral agreements are by far better the better alternative. They take less time to negotiate and far superior to enforce when a dispute arises.

I admonish China to abandon its tariffs on American goods and behave like a financial superpower which it is now rather than taking cover under the ill-gotten label of a "developing country" when it joined the WTO two decades ago.

However China has not made any changes to ameliorate its exploitation of America's intellectual and cultural assets. Chinese Diplomats in the U.S. infiltrated our universities and large cultural events to propagandize Chinese language, culture, and the old paradigm of their Communist Party in addition to stealing fundamental research and development from our institutions.

The U.S. must adopt some of the same techniques it successfully used against the Russian communists in our Cold War against USSR and won. Limit the proliferation of Chinese Diplomatic missions on our soil. Monitor the Chinese Diplomats and their agents against any acts of theft of our intellectual property. Arrest any attempts to spread their Communist propaganda or traits on our people.

CHINA AND AMERICA: WRITINGS 4, 7, 16, 24, 25, 26, 29 AND 30

IN THIS SPECTRUM of writings, I cover the waterfront of issues that have been plaguing America. These include the COVID-19 pandemic that has been ravaging our country beginning in March 2020, the tension of trade tariffs that has been brewing over the last three years, the continued theft of U.S. intellectual property by the Chinese nationals, the violation by China of the WTO treaty and other matters.

In article 24 ("COVID-19: China's Inadvertent WMD") I bluntly pin the origin of the coronavirus in Wuhan, China and for spreading this virus across the world on China. The over 25 million infections and over a million deaths worldwide, as of this writing, because of the coronavirus are attributable to the negligence of the Chinese Community Party; China also controlled the World Health Organization to suppress the place of origin of this disease.

In this article I correctly called the pandemic as China's weapon of mass destruction! In fact, the virus is biological warfare that China unleashed on humanity. China did not have the humility or grace to acknowledge its mistake. Instead, it unfairly attempted to blame the U.S. for causing and spreading this disease.

Unfortunately the coronavirus pandemic and the unfair

tariffs that China imposed on American exports are the root cause for an economic Cold War that is developing between the two countries. Sadly, the pandemic and the Cold War may take a long time to control and bring it to an end.

In the articles 4 and 17 titled "Why does U.S. go to War?" and " A World Without America", respectively I examined the U.S. war machine and the military industrial complex that we built which has been keeping America safe and helping other nations from committing tyranny on their people.

The second article paints a bleak picture of the world without America's presence or participation. Here is an excerpt from this article: *"In general, the new world will be a dark place devoid of the stability and order that the present world is accustomed to. Regional wars will break out without the U.S. serving as a world's cop to maintain law and order. India and Pakistan at the slightest provocation will unleash their nuclear weapons with scant regard for China's influence killing hundreds of millions of their people. The other bitter enemies Iran and Israel will unleash their nuclear might at each other to their mutual destruction. Russia will be helpless in such a conflict despite its expected sphere of influence in the Middle East."*

I wrote this piece to remind that American stands for and strives toward fairness, freedom and liberty for all people in the world.

The article on the economics and politics of oil (#7) is a congratulatory message to America to have finally weaned away from perennial dependence on the Organization of Petroleum Exporting Countries for oil and its determination to become self-sufficient in oil production through fracking. This was deservedly self-congratulatory because we not only produced oil from underneath our rocks through our ingenuity, but also overcame the environmentalists who regularly opposed such production based on false fear of permanent damage to Earth's environment.

In my article #25 ("Is America Stupid–My Conversations with Australians"), written on a lighter note, I narrate the conversations I had with Australians on a cruise ship while travelling from Perth, Australia to Cape Town, South Africa. A conversation in which a retired Australian confronted me with the unexpected and abrupt statement that America is stupid. His statement motivated me to explore the truth in what he said and find answers. *"While America is techno-logically superior and we boast how smart we are as a nation, I discovered that when it comes to politics, we are gullible and believe what we are fed by the news media."* Perhaps every nation has its share of stupid people.

In the remaining articles I wrote about our domestic political situation of utter polarization between the present ruling and opposition parties in our country and suggest ways of reaching a compromise and reunify America.

The dramatic change in our habits brought by the coro-navirus epidemic of working from home by relying on technology to conduct business was the subject matter of another of my writings (# 27) titled "Work from Home is an Enduring Shift that Businesses should Embrace". Many businesses consider this change is better for their bottom-line profits. The employees living in high population areas such as the Silicon Valley and New York City regard this as a time saver from their daily commute to work and increase their productivity.

The article on "Crisis Drives America" is an accurate observation that America seems to react when a calamity strikes us as opposed to taking precautionary measures in anticipation of it. The ravage that was inflicted by the COVID-19 pandemic is an example of our unpreparedness despite the warning received five years earlier from Microsoft Founder Bill Gates. Our government did not pay heed to this dire warning so much so that when the pandemic happened, we had to scramble for basic protective equipment like ventilators and masks.

Finally I envision a time when the North American countries of Canada, Mexico and the U.S. could merge into a united country called the United States of North America. Such unification solves many problems that these neighbors are now facing and ushers in a new country which would be stronger, richer, self-dependent, self-protected and more peaceful. Such a fairytale tale nation encompassing the entire continent of North America would set a wonderful example for the rest of the world to emulate.

PRAGMATIC ADVICE TO AMERICA

AMERICA CONTINUES TO be the best place of hope, opportunity and freedom. America did not become the world's richest and most powerful country by accident. We reached this singular position because we carried a sense of optimism and had a "can-do" attitude. Other factors contributed to our status including a demography of relatively young population, a geography protected by the Pacific and Atlantic oceans on two sides and friendly neighbors on the other sides, a political system of representative democracy based on three branches of government, an economic system founded on capitalism, a rich history of struggle and success, and the rule of law.

The timeless principles embodied in our Constitution and the accompanying Bill of Rights which gives us freedom of speech, freedom to practice religion without governmental intervention and a government serving to protect our life, liberty and property will remain as pillars of our democracy. Our system of representative democracy is by no means perfect and yet we are the most successful nation on the Earth. We survived foreign invasions and territorial attacks, a Civil War, a Cold War, the Great Depression, and the Great Recession. With compromise, we will emerge triumphant in the political polarization that our country is facing now.

We were the best when it comes to innovation and our

free-enterprise economic principles contributed to entrepreneurism and served us well. However, we are beginning to
slip in holding on to our top ranking in U.S. patents.

We are not the best when it comes to offering the best
education to our children. We have been static in our K-12
education for decades and a lot needs to be done to improve
it. We need to return to teaching our children civics and history without distorting it. To continue our nation's innovation
and entrepreneurism, we should place more emphasis on
teaching the subjects of STEM. This will entail our youngsters
to find rewarding jobs when they grow up and fortify our
middle-class which has been the backbone of our nation.

We should find a cure for the virus of teachers' unions
which infected our education system. The value that the
unions add is little, but they drain our teachers of their
resources. The forced annual dues upon which the union
leadership survives have captivated our teachers and abridged
their first Amendment right of free speech. We should return
to the days when such union did not exist and the teachers
performed better by imparting true American values through
proper education to the students.

Our institutions of higher education continue to be the
best and attract foreign students. We award more PhD degrees to foreigners than to Americans. With this immense
investment that our academic institutions make in foreign
graduates, our immigration laws warrant changes so as to

retain these awardees permanently in the U.S. and enrich our country through more innovation and entrepreneurship.

The muggy atmosphere that has been created on our university campuses to impinge on or to suppress free speech should be ended. Free speech on campus, even if it is political speech, needs protection when one side disagrees robustly, even fiercely. Robust civil discourse is part of the campus learning experience in our civil society.

This requires our professors to offer a balanced education as opposed to indoctrinating students toward their one-sided radical leftist viewpoints. The university administrators have a duty to promote free speech on their campus, particularly when their institution received tax-payer funding, without which the very existence of the university may be in jeopardy.

Likewise, social media companies which are behaving like news media and promoting only liberal leaning should be cognizant of the governmental immunity offered to them. Balance and fairness is expected of them. Or else, they may lose such protection and will be exposed from their behavior to multi-million-dollar lawsuits from victims who suffered abridgement of their privacy and free speech rights.

Another problem with our educational institutions at the pre-college and university levels is a bloated administration that now exists to manage education. This is a drain on taxpayers' resources who through property taxes subsidize the public institutions and parents who pay tuition for their enrolled children. Such bureaucracy is a waste, adds little value to education and should be pared.

Our multinational corporations should demonstrate their allegiance to our nation which is now lacking. Corporations are governed by the basic principle of a fiduciary duty as established by their stockholders. The fiduciary duty includes legal, ethical, and economic responsibilities. Overlapping these is the unwritten duty of corporate citizenship, which involves social, moral and community responsibilities to the country where they are incorporated.

Outsourcing of U.S. jobs to foreign countries to generate higher profits is not an act of corporate citizenship. In this regard shareholders and corporate officers have an important role to play. Just like we expect our citizens to show patriotism and loyalty to our country, the shareholders and officers should take the corporate bull by the horns and put the company they own on the path to meet its corporate citizenship responsibilities as an indispensable part of the fiduciary duty.

We should not be complacent when it comes to our never-ending influx of illegal aliens. We should be imaginative in curbing it not only by establishing an impenetrable border wall, but also work with the governments in Mexico, Central and South America to find ways of keeping those foreign citizens in their home countries through productive employment and ensuring that their freedoms are restored.

One potential solution is to cooperate with these governments and establish the supply chains that American industry would need as we distance our dependence on China.

On the high stakes tension brewing between the U.S. and China ignited by the trade tariffs, the U.S. should steadfastly continue the actions that have been boldly initiated by President Trump. Tightening export controls against China, enhancing investment screening, challenging Chinese technology companies, and blunting the Belt and Road Initiative of China are weapons of choice that the U.S. should continue to use.

Today China poses not only an economic, but also a military threat to America's future. The policy of appeasement towards China that is advocated by the leftist Democratic Party would not work. China wants to replace the world's reserve currency of the U.S. dollar with its yuan. Its ultimate goal is to become the military superpower by dethroning America's from its present military title.

Historically China is a country that cannot be trusted. It is reckless and deceptive and would go to any length to steal our technology as the American private and public sectors realized over the past three decades.

A continued confrontation at the governmental level is necessary for China to pay heed to our trade demands which are fair and well justified. In pressuring the Chinese Communist Party, we should continue to show quiet courage in our beliefs and the rule of law. If this does not produce the results, we should decouple our economy from the Chinese economy.

We should promote and support a military alliance in the Asia Pacific comprised of Japan, India and Australia to deter China's hegemony in the South China Sea and the Indian Ocean.

We should break the bonds of the unholy alliance that now exists between the Chinese Communist Party and its billionaire oligarchs. We should put our arm around these oligarchs who amassed their wealth by stealing our technology and siphoning off our investments in China so they would silently persuade the CCP to loosen its grip on totalitarianism and become a respectable member of the world community.

On the military front, America should never again engage in optional wars. We should continue to invest in our military and be fully prepared and capable of defending our country from foreign attacks. As has been said, "Eternal vigilance is the price of liberty!" We should engage our National Security Administration and the Central Intelligence Agency to be vigilant to gain advance intelligence to forestall any surprise attack, whether military, cyber or other and thwart it before it happen.

America should continue to fulfill the responsibility thrust on us as a global power. We are indispensable to the world. International problems cannot be addressed successfully without our leadership. The power of our military has been an indispensable contributor for maintaining world peace and must remain so. However, we should not assume the role of a cop to address every act of aggression or every crisis external to our borders.

We should rebuild and modernize our infrastructure of roads, bridges, dams, communication networks, power grids, mass transportation, and fresh water delivery systems etc. which have been neglected for well over half century. Despite our energy self-sufficiency through fracking, we should accelerate our transition from dependence on fossil fuels to clean energy. Such inward focus is not only necessary, but imperative for us to survive in the 21st century and continue to remain as the superpower. We should continue to remain as the beacon of hope for the rest of the world. We should continue to set an example for other nations to emulate us.

IN CLOSING

Domestically America is now at a crossroads. The state of our nation is alarming and many Americans are concerned that the America that they knew and lived in for decades may cease to exist.

Marxism, socialism and anarchy are terrorizing our streets and threatening the values that made America the greatest nation on earth. The Democratic Party is unwilling to speak against these threats. With their silence in effect they are embracing these principles which are alien to our country. History has demonstrated that these principles failed in other countries and brought poverty and misery to their people.

The most compelling problem our nation is facing now is political polarization between members of the Democratic and Republican parties in U.S. Congress. High unemployment, economic recovery, ending the coronavirus pandemic and dealing with China on trade matters are the other challenges our nation is facing.

There is no rule book for how America to manage these challenges. Even our mighty think tanks have not written such rule book.

What is needed to manage these challenges is simple common sense. The President, Congress and Judiciary need to recognize that the stakes are high. They should work together by putting the country and its citizenry at the forefront. They need to build mutual trust, discuss openly by talking through, finding creative solutions to the obstacles and sincerely negotiate to resolve them.

The political polarization that beset us requires compromise by giving something in return for something else. This is how trust is established. It is going to be a rocky start. The ride to compromise is not going to be smooth, but if we work together with the American "can-do" spirit, we will succeed.

By putting the country first and setting aside our personal egos, we will be able to create a perfect bridge between what had been and what was to come. This recipe is bound to rejuvenate America to the glory days of free enterprise, limited government and traditional American values.

In time America will find a vaccine against the coronavirus which will free us from the chains of confinement that tied us up. The unexpected national quarantine and the sudden self-generated set back of our economy, which was firing on all cylinders before the pandemic stuck us, will bounce back. With the repatriation of trillions of dollars of profits generated overseas, our private sector will make America into the high-tech manufacturing superpower and create high-paying jobs for every American.

America has won a Cold War in the past. In due course we will win the present economic Cold War with China and the trade tensions will cool off. If not, America will go on its own and become self-dependent. Or we will establish alternative supply chains and trade with other nations, particularly Mexico and Canada by fully implementing the USMCA and other (bilateral) agreements. That will spell the economic death knell for China.

I believe in the words of wisdom uttered by Warren Buffet, who is now a 90-year-old nonagenarian, while talking about America in the time of the coronavirus. He said: *"Nothing can stop America when you come down to it, even with the scariest of scenarios. It may have been tested during the Great Depression, and it may be tested now to some degree.*

In the end the answer is never bet against America. That in my view is true today as it was in 1789 and even was true during the Civil War and the depths of depression."

I admire Buffet's genuine optimism in America. With a strong belief in American values, I believe we will reemerge as the most powerful country once again and continue to remain as the exceptional nation on the Earth.

President Trump when accepting his nomination for a second term as the 2020 Republican presidential candidate described America this way: *"We are a nation of pilgrims, pioneers, adventurers, explorers and trail-blazers who refused to be tied down or reined in. Americans have steel in their spines, grit in their souls, and fire in their hearts. There is no one like us on earth."*

I wholeheartedly agree with the President's assessment of America.

ABOUT THE AUTHOR

THE AUTHOR HAS a rare combination of multi-disciplined education, a kaleidoscopic professional career and rich cultural background. His first love of physics drove him to the pinnacle of leaning of physics, as evidenced by the degrees he earned which include a B.S., M.S., M. A., and Ph.D.

While working as a physics teacher and later as a physicist at General Dynamics Corporation, T.R. pursued law to earn his J.D. and synergistically combine his scientific background with the knowledge of law and became an American Intellectual Property attorney. T.R. has been admitted to practice in New York, Ohio, Vermont, and the United States Patent Bar. Additionally. he is admitted to practice before Court of Appeals for the Federal Circuit and the Supreme Court of the United States.

Before serving as the Vice President and Chief Intellectual Property Law Counsel at International Game Technology Corp. he championed patent licensing and litigation as a Senior Director at NVIDIA Corporation. Prior to that, T.R. spearheaded as a Corporate Executive IP Counsel at IBM for over two decades. At IBM he orchestrated many Executive and Senior management positions in many world locations including a five-year international assignment as the Assistant General Counsel in charge of IP in IBM's Asia Pacific

Headquarters in Tokyo. Prior to IBM, he capitalized as a Patent Lawyer at NCR Corporation and as a Senior Research Engineer at General Dynamics Corporation.

Of Indian heritage, T.R. has gainfully combined his rich and disciplined Indian cultural upbringing with the consensus building of the Japanese that he was exposed to while living in Japan and the competitive, innovative and can-do work ethic prevalent in the United States.

T.R. presented and published over fifty papers and talks on physics, intellectual property, and on corporate law matters, including contributing a chapter on the Semiconductor Chip Protection Act to the legal treatise of *Intellectual Property Litigation & Licensing*. He served for three years on the Editorial Board of the *AIPLA Quarterly Journal* of the American Intellectual Property Law Association. In April 2020 he chronicled his life in the title *The Green Card Dowry Plan* published by Ingram Spark.

T.R.'s kaleidoscopic work experience has been as a physics teacher, physicist, software architect, intellectual property attorney, patent license specialist and litigator, public speaker, mentor and writer.

www.ingramcontent.com/pod-product-compliance
Lightning Source LLC
Chambersburg PA
CBHW060316030426
42336CB00011B/1078